AL
4.60

W9-DHK-253

CHARACTER IN ENGLISH LITERATURE

Character
in English Literature

By

CHRISTOPHER GILLIE

1967
CHATTO & WINDUS
LONDON

Published by
Chatto and Windus Ltd
42 William IV Street
London W.C.2

*

Clarke, Irwin & Co Ltd
Toronto

First published 1965
Reprinted 1967

PRINTED IN GREAT BRITAIN BY
WILLIAM LEWIS (PRINTERS) LTD., CARDIFF

For Margery

ACKNOWLEDGEMENT

I would like to record my gratitude to Brian Jackson for the ungrudging encouragement and criticism he has accorded me in the writing of this book.

C.G.

i

Contents

INTRODUCTION: Character and the Reader   *page* 9

Part 1: Character as Role in Ritual

CHAPTER

1 MAN AND HIS UNIVERSE: Everyman ·
Sir Gawayn and the Green Knight   27

2 WOMEN BY CHAUCER: The Wife of Bath ·
Criseyde   41

3 KINGS: A Study of *Macbeth*   56

4 LOVERS BY SHAKESPEARE:
Anthony and Cleopatra   71

Part 2: The Emergence of Loneliness

5 MILTON'S SATAN   89

6 THE PICARESQUE HERO:
Christian · Crusoe   101

Part 3: Character and Society

7 THE HEROINE VICTIM
1: Emma Woodhouse · Catherine Earnshaw   117

8 THE HEROINE VICTIM
2: Gwendolen Harleth · Isabel Archer   135

9 CHARACTER AND ENVIRONMENT:
Pip of *Great Expectations* ·
Henchard of *The Mayor of Casterbridge*   156

10 HUMAN SUBJECT AND HUMAN SUB-
STANCE: Dedalus of *A Portrait of the Artist* ·
Birkin of *Women in Love*   177

INDEX

Introduction

CHARACTER AND THE READER

I. LIVING WITH THE ALIEN

WHY do we like to read about imaginary people?

Once upon a time there were four little Rabbits, and their names were – Flopsy, Mopsy, Cotton-tail and Peter. They lived with their Mother in a sand-bank, underneath the root of a very big fir-tree. 'Now, my dears,' said old Mrs Rabbit one morning, 'you may go into the fields or down the lane, but don't go into Mr McGregor's garden: your Father had an accident there: he was put in a pie by Mrs McGregor. Now run along, and don't get into mischief. I am going out.' Then old Mrs Rabbit took a basket and her umbrella, and went through the wood to the baker's. She bought a loaf of brown bread and five currant buns. Flopsy, Mopsy, and Cotton-tail, who were good little bunnies, went down the lane to collect blackberries: but Peter, who was very naughty, ran straight away to Mr McGregor's garden, and squeezed under the gate!

This will be recognised as the opening of one of the earliest stories in the experience of many of us, and it is a small masterpiece. Let us see what it can show us about character. The family is one of rabbits, who are also children; there is no difficulty about this dual role – we never forget that they are both, and the illustrations greatly help us to remember. We also have villains in the piece – Mr and Mrs McGregor – but they are a gardener and his wife, and gardeners are not sinister. There is nothing evidently frightening about the story therefore: rabbits and gardeners are both comfortable things, at least to infants. And yet the story has a backdoor into excitement since the rabbits are also children: three of them are good, one of them is naughty. If you are good you pick blackberries, which is nice; but if you are naughty you have adventures, which is much nicer – at any rate before you have them – Peter Rabbit barely escapes with his life.

It is important to notice in the story that naughtiness is involved with adventures, and adventure with what is alien. To the infant much of the world is alien and therefore dangerous, but he supposes that as he grows it will become familiar and therefore safe; to some extent he is right. In the meantime if he could analyse his experience he might discover that when the alien does not transform itself into the familiar, it may either persist as the incorrigibly frustrating, or – like Mr McGregor – as the actively but comprehensibly malevolent; or it may persist as the incomprehensibly evil.

The incomprehensible is best dealt with by folk tale, fairy story and myth. *Little Red Riding Hood* gives the infant evil in an acceptable form: since there must be bad things, it is easy to understand that a wolf is one. It is less easy to understand witches, but since people are also, sometimes, incomprehensibly bad, witch-hood is a handy way of summarising the fact. In *Snow White* he will face the further mystery that what is bad is not necessarily ugly, though not as beautiful as the good (Snow White) and always more like itself if it can make itself ugly, as the witch-stepmother can. The child grows a little, but the incomprehensibly alien and intrinsically evil still challenge him; he graduates to Greek myth, Arthurian romance, or, if a semblance of reality has become necessary to him, Wild Westerns. Cowboys or gods, we notice that in all such mythology character displays itself as role: princess, gunman, witch or pirate present no surprises, for all that we need to know of them is labelled upon them on introduction. Such characters are not necessarily dull nor nearly so simple as they may appear; we shall return to character as role. But as we shall see, modern myth cannot express modern experience: the more up to date the myth, the cruder. The intelligent child, whether or not he instinctively understands this, will become interested in stories that have the flavour, and kind of complexity, of actual life. Fantasy may be mixed with the fact, but the distinction has become important to him and the relationship of the two must somehow be made plain. Much of his reading will be about ordinary children having reasonable adventures.

One such tale – a children's classic if a minor one – is *The*

INTRODUCTION

Story of the Treasure Seekers by E. Nesbit. In this story six children set about trying to restore the fortunes of their family. The facts are vague to them: 'Father was very ill after Mother died; and while he was ill his business-partner went to Spain – and there was never much money afterwards. I don't know why.' The adventures that follow are those of children who are normally naughty – that is to say enterprising – but have a strong moral sense. This moral sense is important, for while it complicates the adventures, it makes both them and the children more meaningful. The adventures are funny, for they bring the children again and again up against the alien world of adults, who always misunderstand and are always misunderstood. When, remarkably enough, their enterprise is at last successful, it is in result of an episode in which the children have no thought of it. A maternal uncle comes to talk business; as usual the children misunderstand what is implied, but the reader infers distinctly that the uncle has rich commercial interests in India, that in consequence the father is seeking his help, that he dis-approves of the father, and that their unsatisfactory interview ends in his decision not to throw good money after bad. The children, on the other hand, suppose that the uncle is a real Indian and deduce that he must be poor, for they have had to learn the passage that contains the phrase 'Lo the poor Indian'. They therefore feel sorry for him (despite his rudeness) and altruistically resolve to help him.

As the poor Indian came down our steps he saw me there at the gate. I did not mind his being poor, and I said, 'Good evening, Uncle,' just as politely as though he had been about to ascend into one of the gilded chariots of the rich and affluent, instead of having to walk to the station a quarter of a mile in the mud, unless he had the money for a tram fare.

'Good evening, Uncle.' I said it again, for he stood staring at me. I don't suppose he was used to politeness from boys – some boys are anything but – especially to the Aged Poor.

So I said 'Good evening, Uncle,' yet once again. Then he said –

'Time you were in bed, young man. Eh! – what?'

Then I saw I must speak plainly with him, man to man. So I did. I said –

'You've been dining with my Father, and we couldn't help hearing you say the dinner was shocking. So we thought as you're an Indian, perhaps you're very poor . . . because of "Lo, the poor Indian" – you know – and you can't get a good dinner every day. And we are very sorry if you're poor; and won't you come and have dinner with us tomorrow – with us children, I mean? It's a very, very good dinner – rabbit, and hardbake, and coconut – and you needn't mind us knowing you're poor, because we know honourable poverty is no disgrace, and –' I could have gone on much longer, but he interrupted me to say –

'Upon my word! And what's *your* name, eh?'

'Oswald Bastable,' I said. . . .

'Oswald Bastable, eh? Bless my soul!' said the poor Indian. 'Yes, I'll dine with you, Mr Oswald Bastable, with all the pleasure in life. Very kind and cordial invitation, I'm sure. Good-night, sir. At one o'clock, I presume?'

'Yes, at one,' I said. 'Good-night, sir.'

Then I went in and told the others, and we wrote a paper and put it on the boys' dressing table, and it said –

'The poor Indian is coming at one. He seemed very grateful to me for my kindness.'

So the uncle is shocked out of his complacent meanness by the uncalculating kindness of the uncomprehending children; the father is re-established.

The story is again a comfortable one; moreover, the ending runs close to sentimentality, and the naïvety of the children – Oswald is twelve – is by modern standards unlikely. But the tale has character for two reasons. First, the children are real; notice, for instance, the deliberate hint of slight smugness in Oswald's tone, especially in the last sentence; it piquantly echoes the uncle's own brand, harsh and grown-up as that is. Oswald is as pleased with himself for doing good as the uncle has been with his own financial prudence. Secondly, without moving outside the childish horizon, we are shown the two worlds, childish and adult, in clear relationship, the former as mistakenly assured of its impulses as the latter is of its calculations, which leave it, as we glimpse, pretty much at a loss with itself. The alien is again the condition of the theme; without it the story could not happen nor the characters have their full appeal.

INTRODUCTION

Before he has finished with E. Nesbit, Arthur Ransome, and such writers aiming at his age-group, the enterprising child – he is apt to be called 'bookish' – will feel that it is time to experiment in adult literature. The perplexed parent will often hand him – still more often her – Charlotte Brontë's *Jane Eyre*.

There was no possibility of taking a walk that day. We had been wandering, indeed, in the leafless shrubbery an hour in the morning; but since dinner . . . the cold winter wind had brought with it clouds so sombre, and a rain so penetrating, that further outdoor exercise was now out of the question.

I was glad of it; I never liked long walks, especially on chilly afternoons; dreadful to me was the coming home in the raw twilight, with nipped fingers and toes, and a heart saddened by the chidings of Bessie, the nurse, and humbled by the consciousness of my physical inferiority to Eliza, John, and Georgiana Reed.

The said Eliza, John, and Georgiana were now clustered round their mamma in the drawing-room: she lay reclined on a sofa by the fireside, and with her darlings about her (for the time neither quarrelling nor crying) looked perfectly happy. Me she dispensed from joining the group, saying she regretted to be under the necessity of keeping me at a distance; but that until she heard from Bessie, and could discover by her own observation that I was endeavouring in good earnest to acquire a more sociable and child-like disposition, a more attractive and sprightly manner – something lighter, franker, more natural, as it were – she really must exclude me from privileges intended only for contented, happy little children.

'What does Bessie say I have done?' I asked.

'Jane, I don't like cavillers or questioners; besides, there is something truly forbidding in a child taking up their elders in that manner. Be seated somewhere; and until you can speak pleasantly, remain silent.'

In these opening lines the reader meets the alien in a new way. Jane finds the world strange and unfriendly because this is what she is found to be herself; it is the familiar theme of the Ugly Duckling, or that rather different theme of Cinderella, and indeed, though Jane is no cygnet, she is to find her Prince.

He had a dark face, with stern features and a heavy brow; his eyes and gathered eyebrows looked thwarted and ireful just now.

He was past youth, but had not reached middle age; perhaps he might be thirty-five. Had he been a handsome, heroic-looking gentleman, I should not have dared to stand thus questioning him against his will, and offering my services unasked. I had hardly ever seen a handsome youth; never in my life spoken to one. I had a theoretical reverence and homage for beauty, elegance, gallantry, fascination; but had I met those qualities incarnate in masculine shape, I should have known instinctively that they neither had nor could have sympathy with anything in me, and should have shunned them as one would fire, lightning, or anything else that is bright but antipathetic.

This second passage, where unbeknownst she first encounters her employer, fallen from his horse, has anticipations in the first. Shut out from the golden circle of the fireside in her childhood, Jane remains shut out for all her youth; she accepts exclusion as an unalterable feature of her existence. But the question which Mrs Reed finds so pert – 'What does Bessie say I have done?' – is her self-justification. She does not repine, but she is not cowed; her forsakenness, whatever Mrs Reed may say, is not her fault. So Jane's very diffidence becomes a sort of sturdiness; her limitations become assets, and, self-effacing where others would be forthcoming, she is also undismayed in situations which would in others arouse consternation.

The Tale of Peter Rabbit is an infant's book, and shows the brightly spotlit patch which is the infant world; the alien realm of 'naughtiness', adventure, and danger lies very near, but is itself not large – not larger than Mr McGregor's garden. As the child grows, the patch of familiarity grows too, but even faster; so does the alien world, and faster still, and now the two worlds are intermingled. Thus the Bastable children of *The Treasure Seekers* have the freedom of a considerable territory, and yet the grown-ups loom over them at every step they take. But *Jane Eyre* is an adult book, for Jane learns early that the alien enters into her own being; that she is as alien to the world as the world is to her. She has to learn how to assess herself as she assesses others, interdependent processes which begin on the first page. There we watch her recognising her own disadvantages, but she recognises those of Mrs Reed too. Mrs Reed, on the other hand, lacks the capacity to scrutinise herself and so understands no one else. Where, then, the children's tale has a single dimension – the self (unexplored) exploring what is not the self – the adult tale is three-dimensional: the self is explored, and so is what is not the self, and so is the relationship between these.

Can we now give an answer to the question on the first page: why do we like to read about imaginary people? Fiction may of course help us to 'know' the world better – to familiarise ourselves with its less familiar aspects. It may help us to understand human nature imaginatively through the insights of the great imaginative writers. However, it is a common misconception to suppose that art merely describes its themes; that it presents us with experience at second hand. Great art – and that form of it which is great fiction – is direct experience; that is to say it was lived by its creator, and has to be lived by us if we are to do it justice. The difference between art and life is that the former is articulated – presented as parts in relationship. What possesses relationship can receive it; we can relate ourselves to a work of art, and give form to our own experience by doing so. The alien is the element in which we have existed ever since the womb. True art will not alter its nature, but it may help us to accept it as the condition in which that existence is to become meaningful, if at all.

2. FICTION AS DOPE

But a reader may retort that though this may stand as a description of the way in which he *ought* to read fictions, it by no means truly answers the question of why he wants to. 'I read for entertainment,' he may say; 'for distraction, for relaxation, for escape.' We should notice that, understood in the right way, these are no bad reasons. 'To entertain' in its original sense means something not so very far from 'to sustain'; do we not still 'entertain an opinion'? And we need to 'relax' from the tensions and constrictions with which our private worries and preoccupations afflict us; we need 'distraction' from them, to 'escape'. All this is good, if the distraction is towards something important, if the escape is into greater scope. In these senses, none of these words implies a barrier to the experience of great literature; on the contrary, they suggest an openness to it, a willingness to receive it. The obstacle to literature only begins when such terms are given a different sense; when a reader is really seeking stupefaction and oblivion; when fiction is for him a kind of dope.

What kind of fiction? And what kind of dope? Comparatively few writers, I think, set out to write dope. The dope element in fiction more often arises partly from defects in the writer, and partly from the approach by the reader. On the one side, not many writers succeed in being completely creative in their work; the story gets diverted into the shallows of wishfulness – either the writer's, or what the writer may suppose to be the reader's. Even a novel so good as *Jane Eyre*. for instance, has its wishful element, when Jane-Cinderella overcomes and then wins her prince-ogre, Mr Rochester, although the strength of the book is such that it sets its own criterion, by which we can discern its own weaknesses. Among great writers, Dickens is notorious for the extent to which he caters to the wishfulness of his readers. On the reader's side, almost any book can be read wishfully, if the reader looks in it only for what soothes his nerves, com-pensates for his private frustrations, or satisfies his need for vicarious excitement. Approached in this way, Jane Austen becomes a sedative for old ladies, Emily Brontë a romance for school-girls, and Dickens is admired for his light comedy and melodrama.

A good example of fiction written as dope I take to be such broadcast programmes as 'Mrs Dale's Diary' and 'The Archers'; however, I can only speak of the latter from direct experience. Both purport to record daily life among ordinary people. The characters are presented realistically enough to give listeners the illusion that they are actual, and yet they are unreal enough never to become deeply or in any case permanently involved in tragedy; nor do they have points of view or feelings that could perplex or disturb any listener after the first superficial en-counter. Their world is thus the listener's world, with the difference that the discomfort, difficulty and grief that every listener knows is evident only in the way that a chemical flavouring and bright colouring matter gives individuality to a cheap boiled sweet. The listener can escape into this world without feeling that life is being left behind, while safely aware that he will never encounter his own true image there, complete with warts and skeletons in cupboards. The programme is a mirror, but one which reflects selectively what the onlooker wishes to perceive.

Another such fiction of equal popularity is the British Royal Family as it is presented in the press. The immense utility of such an institution is that it alone can give the illusion of the exceptional which is at the same time the usual: the family is so far exalted above other families as to be mysterious as no other family can be – and at the same time is so ordinary (in its press manifestations) that it is thoroughly accessible. To be a King or Queen is to be a walking romance; but if the Queen loves dogs or the King collects stamps, it is as though after all romance has been sized to our measure. What the people who make up our Royal Family are really like to talk to and live with, very few are in a position to know; but we all have the feeling that we know, and it is this illusion, nurtured by publicity, that constitutes the fiction. An eternally circulating anecdote about the Queen Mother tells how she expressed delight that Maude has had a baby. Wonderment among the listeners: what or which Maude in the Royal Family? Not in the Royal Family at all, it turns out; the Queen Mother has been following 'Mrs Dale's Diary'. This story has been inspired, I think, by an impulse to instal the two most popular British fictions in one enclosure.

3. THE FICTION OF RITUAL

Dope fiction, I suggest then – or any fiction when it is treated as dope – seeks to reconcile its audience to their environment by extracting from that environment what is alien, disagreeable, unacceptable, and substituting what is soothing or titillating – at all events, what is wished. In an age in which religion, even when it is accepted, has commonly lost the power to make the alien universe comprehensively meaningful, such fictions sometimes have the force of religion substitutes, not because they give meaning to the lives of their publics but because they disperse from the minds of these publics the urgency to seek any.

Serious fiction seriously received, on the contrary, is concerned with just this alien quantity that dope excludes; it reconciles us precisely to that, by making us feel it, or enlarging our feeling of it, as the inescapable condition for truthful living.

Fiction does this by presenting an image – an image, commonly, of a character living in tension with alien quantities in his experience. In our civilisation, however, we share few except superficial common assumptions; writers are instinctively or consciously aware of this limitation, and on the whole offer us 'realistic' images – that is to say, images which, initially at least, represent particular people undergoing experiences appropriate to them. A modern Everyman, undergoing experience common to all men, would either be so superficial as to be uninteresting, or so complex as to be all but unintelligible, although James Joyce's *Finnegans Wake* is perhaps an attempt to present just such a figure. This does not mean that modern fiction cannot have a general appeal; we can say what interests us about a character, and why this should interest a great many people, but we cannot say that it is the truth about everybody.

Once, however, artists were comparatively unrestricted by such limitations. Religions had true binding power and offered cosmic visions which were the assumptions of all or most in a society; Everyman had a reality, and death was not merely a separate lonely experience for each, but one which had a common significance for all. 'Religion', admittedly, must not be taken simply here: religions have a way of overlaying each other, so that an obsolete one still maintains hold on the imagination, as forms of paganism did under medieval Christianity, revealing themselves in poems of old half-Christianised legends, and even in the miracle plays. Moreover, pseudo-religions arise to satisfy impulses which the prevailing form seems to ignore or deny; so arose the courtly code of romantic love, and the legends of great lovers, because the Church's view of carnal appetite combined with the secular view of the social function of marriage to frustrate the passions. But whether a religion be orthodox, heretical, obsolete or synthetic, it is important for literary study if it enables the whole of a society or at least whole classes in one to accept representative

INTRODUCTION

images for whole ranges of experience. Such are the images of ritual, representing, or rather embodying and realising, widely held and profoundly felt assumptions about human nature and its hopes, fears, desires and destiny.

Ritual images in the form of characters exist to play fore-ordained roles, much as in fairy stories, and as any one fairy tale is likely to be a version of another, so writers seldom invented their fictions but gave new forms to tales which often had a long history. This did not prevent the tales having variety and the characters individuality. The writer brought to bear on his theme unique qualities of his own temperament, society and time; moreover, these qualities might well include peculiar doubts about or special versions of prevailing beliefs; in addition each character would possess not only the individuality afforded him by his role but might be further complicated by a mixture of roles, as Hamlet is a scholar as well as a prince. Nevertheless, the more deeply one inquires into a medieval or Renaissance character, the more universal his nature becomes; he is a version of Everyman sharing Everyman's universe, and he draws his vitality from this deep common source. The alien quantity of experience is known and felt as such by all. In nineteenth- and twentieth-century fiction, on the other hand, characters draw together at their surfaces but in their depths each lives apart; the alien quantity is the private predicament.

4. RITUALISM INTO REALISM

How did the 'ritualistic fiction' of the Middle Ages and the Renaissance modify into modern realistic fiction?

The Jacobean dramatists – Shakespeare, Jonson, Middleton, Tourneur, Webster, Ford – wrote between lights. From the past, the medieval cosmos, in its nature friendly to Man yet alienated from him by his Fall, threw long shadows: characters still stalked, with an increasing sense of their incongruity, through pre-ordained roles. Over against this steady, fading light rose others, flickering, uncertain: reason acknowledging its own dimness; the passions – especially the economic ones; the Commonweal or Society, uncertain of its principles of cohesion, if it is not gain. So Hamlet on Man:

I have of late – but wherefore I know not – lost all my mirth, foregone all custom of exercises; and, indeed, it goes so heavily with my disposition that this goodly frame, the earth, seems to me a sterile promontory; this most excellent canopy the air, look you, this brave o'erhanging firmament, this majestical roof fretted with golden fire, – why, it appears no other thing to me than a foul and pestilent congregation of vapours. What a piece of work is man! how noble in reason! how infinite in faculty! in form and moving how express and admirable! in action how like an angel! in apprehension how like a god! the beauty of the world! the paragon of animals! And yet, to me, what is this quintessence of dust? man delights not me; no, nor woman neither, though by your smiling you seem to say so.

'The time is out of joint: – O cursed spite, That ever I was born to set it right!' The Court of Denmark is not an unfair image of the morally inert society, governed by expediency, that was coming into existence.

So the century saw interest in psychology, and produced Burton's *Anatomy of Melancholy*; it developed a more empirical interest in political authority, and we have Hobbes' *Leviathan*. Light-heartedly, men were dressed up in their psychological and social types by John Earle (of *Microcosmographie*) and others, and social behaviour became the subject of the Restoration Comedy of Manners; more seriously, real individuals were perceptively and graphically delineated by biographers such as Aubrey and historians such as Clarendon, and Dryden's satirical portraiture showed a new command of the medium. Freshness and concision had been found before, but not this agility, this familiarity with human contradictions in, to take an example, the following description of the Earl of Shaftesbury:

> For close Designs and crooked Counsels fit,
> Sagacious, Bold, and Turbulent of wit,
> Restless, unfixt in Principles and Place,
> In Pow'r unpleased, impatient of Disgrace;
> A fiery Soul, which working out its way,
> Fretted the Pigmy Body to decay:
> And o'er informed the Tenement of Clay.
> A daring Pilot in extremity;
> Pleas'd with the Danger, when the Waves went high

He sought the Storms; but, for a Calm unfit,
Would Steer too nigh the Sands to boast his Wit.
Great Wits are sure to Madness near alli'd
And thin Partitions do their Bounds divide;
Else, why should he, with Wealth and Honour blest,
Refuse his Age the needful hours of Rest?
Punish a Body which he coud not please,
Bankrupt of Life, yet Prodigal of Ease?
And all to leave what with his Toil he won
To that unfeather'd two-legged thing a Son:
Got, while his Soul did huddled Notions trie;
And born a shapeless Lump, like Anarchy.
In Friendship false, implacable in Hate,
Resolv'd to Ruine or to Rule the State;
To Compass this the Triple Bond he broke;
The Pillars of the Publick Safety shook,
And fitted *Israel* for a Foreign Yoke;
Then, seized with Fear, yet still affecting Fame,
Usurp'd a Patriot's All-attoning Name.

The Elizabethan Machiavellian character, started by Marlowe and Kyd on the basis of what they supposed to be the Italian philosopher's prescription, feared neither God nor Man and cared for nothing but his own designs; in style of presentation he varied from the violent grotesque of Marlowe's Jew of Malta to the only too plausible Antonio of Shakespeare's *Tempest*. But subtly presented or blatantly, he was always the diametric opposite to what a man ought to be; he was a monster, somewhat equivalent to a modern psychopath. Dryden's portrait of Shaftesbury (called Achitophel in the poem) shows a more fearful because at once a more intelligible and more unpredictable figure. The Elizabethan Machiavellian contained himself – 'I am myself alone,' says Richard of Gloucester in Shakespeare's *Henry VI* – and such unnatural composure in evil makes him more diabolic than human, and more credible therefore to a generation that believed naturally in 'the Evil One' without inquiring too closely into his nature. Once a Machiavellian has set his course, nothing will deter him from it: he is as assured as the saint. Shaftsbury's 'fiery Soul' is not less relentless, but 'working out its way' it destroys the man as he

21

destroys the state. Willy-nilly, Shaftsbury has to make violence his element, not because he is committed to evil but because his energy consumes him. Unlike the Machiavellian, he has no set course, for it is contrary to his nature to be consistent in principle, policy, or even self-interest.

The portrait is incisive, but the appraisal is cool; regarded as a destructive force, Shaftesbury is demonstrated in all his menace; regarding him as a man, Dryden rather shows what emotions it is possible to feel for him than demonstrates these feelings himself. Shaftesbury, in one light, can be pitied; in another, despised; but in a third, he must be admired. His destructiveness to the ordered framework of the state derives from his greatness – is, paradoxically, the quality of a virtue. One remembers the saying of Keats: '. . . there is an electric fire in human nature tending to purify – so that among these human creatures there is continually some birth of new heroism'. And again: 'Though a quarrel in the Streets is a thing to be hated, the energies displayed in it are fine; the commonest Man shows a grace in his quarrel. . . .'

Though it was no part of Dryden's purpose to imply a greatness in Shaftesbury that society lacked, one feels that he knew quite well what he was doing when he presented him as a phenomenon that society could not accommodate. Undoubtedly he had in his mind the Miltonic Satan – a much greater figure, though it is doubtful whether Milton knew as well what he was doing when he depicted that menace to cosmic society, for Satan, though he fails to destroy the framework of the cosmos, does obtrude from that of the poem. In short, Dryden understood what Milton showed – that the Devil had got loose. The medieval cosmos, which had had a secure place for him, was broken. Humanity was quickly building a smart new one, from which he was to be shut out; the official tactic was now no longer to confront him, but to ignore him, much as the devils in *Paradise Lost* try to ignore God in the parody of Paradise which they build in Hell. None the less, he was having his revenge, already, and still more in time to come, for if you ignore Evil you are in danger of ignoring Spirit. So the novel arose early in the eighteenth century, and became, as a modern critic has described it, 'the epic of Man without God'. Not of course that either society or the novel could in fact exclude either God or Satan, but both could deny the Spiritual Powers explicit recognition, while none the less having to endure their permeation.

The radical change in outlook in accordance with which the novel arose can be traced, then, in many forms of literature throughout the seventeenth century. What of the novel form itself? It began as a narrative of loosely connected adventures occurring typically on a journey: the form we call 'picaresque' from the Spanish word 'picaro', a rogue who takes to the road. In the sixteenth century the typical 'picaro' was a social castaway, dislocated from society by the slow collapse of its feudal forms and the disorderly growth of new ones. But there were other forms of castaway. The most notable was the Pilgrim, picking his way out of the earthly society into the heavenly one through a succession of allegories. This was an ancient tradition which Bunyan – whose achievement in it is unmatched – inherited through the pulpit, though he owed much, too, to the more secular kind of romance. But Bunyan's great allegory is not merely a culmination; it is a watershed. On the one hand the book has its traditional and spiritual purpose, but the purpose has changed, since for Bunyan there is no great ecclesiastical hierarchy to mediate between a soul and its salvation, so that his pilgrims are thrown all but desperately on to their own resources. On the other hand, Bunyan has a wide, vivid, sagacious knowledge of this world of man without God, through which a pilgrimage has to be made, as well as a deep understanding of the bewildering variety of the human heart. As a prose narrative about the psychology of human beings in relation to their destinies, *Pilgrim's Progress* was unprecedented in English literature, and to describe the book in such terms is only to describe what was to be the principal concern of the great novelists.

5. CONCLUSION

I hope that what I have said in this Introduction is enough to explain how this book has come to take its shape. I have tried to show that the art of characterisation arises from the sense that at any time between birth and death human experience is confronted by what it feels to be alien – by what it feels to be not merely strange but implicitly dangerous, not to say hostile. From this confrontation issues growth and identity, and the two combine to form character – both the existence of it in the experiencer and his awareness of it in others. Secondly, I have tried to explain my view that characterisation comes into its own only with the novel, for by then – the eighteenth century – the old comprehensive pattern of a universe in whose design the individual could find a place and a meaning in terms of destiny was for ever broken. The new more limited framework, Society, was far less comfortable and subject to endless reconstructions; often it has presented no sort of home for the individual, but only the circumstances of loneliness. With Milton's Satan, *Pilgrim's Progress*, and Robinson Crusoe, the theme of loneliness first enters English literature.

Part 1

Character as Role in Literature

Chapter 1

Man and his Universe
EVERYMAN · THE GREEN KNIGHT

BOTH these works are anonymous and uncertain in date: *Everyman* belongs to the late fifteenth century; *Sir Gawayn and the Green Knight* is about a century older. Both are masterpieces and crucial for the insights they give into the medieval mind, but, for reasons of its greater intelligibility, *Everyman* is much the better known, so we shall discuss that first.

I. EVERYMAN

We do not nowadays talk of Everyman but of the Average Man, a statistical utility who never walks the streets, though we also refer to him as 'the Man in the Street'. Such a figure is useful as a means of generalising about tastes, opinions, hours of work, or standards of living; almost never do we refer to him in connection with human destiny. If we were to say 'the Average Man dies', the statement would either be so obvious as to be quite pointless, or so nonsensical as to seem to imply that if one can rise above the average, one may escape death. But for a medieval to say 'Every man dies' would have been to express the basic drama of human existence, the fundamental human preoccupation. Nowadays, when we think about death, it is chiefly about how to avoid or postpone it, and for most of us what happens after death is anybody's unprofitable guess.

It follows that we do not give much attention to how one should die; such a concern would seem to the 'average man' a morbid and useless one. But since how to die determined for the medieval man what would be his fate after death, pondering the question, far from being useless, was immensely practical and urgent; it was the form of his death, indeed, that gave meaning and form to his whole life. Thus the play *Everyman* is about dying; or, more precisely, about what dying means.

The character of Everyman is of course as generalised as

possible, but unlike our Average Man, he is not abstract. He is made concrete by being shown to be the sort of man who would find it difficult to die. He is, that is to say, neither a very sick nor a miserably poor man, such as might find release in death; nor is he a remarkably good man who could face death with the assurance at least of leaving a good name behind him. He is a sensual man, who has identified himself with the values of this world, – with Fellowship, who represents the cronies of his pleasures; with Cousin and Kindred, who represents his family in alliance of self-interest; above all, with Goods. All these forsake him as he faces his 'long journey'. They even display callousness, and Goods shows a chuckling contempt:

> Marry, thou broughtest thyself in care,
> Whereof I am glad,
> I must needs laugh, I cannot be sad.

Among the personages in the play, Goods has perhaps the most 'character' – the most flavour and force. This is appropriate, for it is in his treatment of worldly wealth that the key to Everyman's predicament above all lies. Goods is shown to be gross, sluggish and unfeeling; but he is only the last by his nature. In himself he is neither good nor bad, but by overvaluing him Everyman has baulked him of the value he might have had, for Goods is meant to be mobile, whereas accumulation has produced in him inertia.

> GOODS: Who calleth me? Everyman? what haste thou hast!
> I lie here in corners, trussed and piled so high
> And in chests I am locked so fast,
> Also sacked in bags, thou mayst see with thine eye,
> I cannot stir; in packs low I lie.

When, in despair, Everyman turns from Goods to his Gooddeeds, he finds that the latter, too, is unable to help him, though unlike the former he is willing:

> Here I lie cold in the ground;
> Thy sins hath me sore bound
> That I cannot stir.

'Cold in the ground' suggests a grave. The chief of Everyman's sins has been avarice; goods are meant to be a means to good deeds, and by themselves amount to mere dead weight. Everyman's error in supposing that they are an end in themselves derives from his root error of imagining his life to be merely his own. But Death, in the course of his summons at the beginning of the play, has told him otherwise:

> DEATH: What, weenest thou thy life is given thee,
> And thy worldly goods also?
> EVERYMAN: I had wend so, verily.
> DEATH: Nay, nay; it was but lent thee;
> For as soon as thou art go,
> Another awhile shall have it, and then go therefro
> Even as thou hast done.
> Everyman, thou art mad; thou hast thy wits five,
> And here on earth will not amend thy life,
> For suddenly I do come.

'Thou art mad.' Not only Death, but Fellowship, Kindred, Cousin and Goods also imply his folly, by the curt off-handedness with which they desert him. The wisdom of this world is not the wisdom of the next, and a man is a fool who supposes that he can confuse means and ends. So Goods tells him in the plainest terms.

The other 'worldly' characters have almost as much flavour as Goods himself. Fellowship, for instance, when first summoned by Everyman, is suave, beguiling and unctuous:

> Everyman, good morrow by this day,
> Sir, why lookest thou so piteously?
> If any thing be amiss, I pray thee, me say,
> That I may help to remedy.

When Everyman expresses his distress, Fellowship promises support even to peril of death:

> Sir, I must needs know your heaviness;
> I have pity to see you in any distress;
> If any you have wronged ye shall revenged be,
> Though I on the ground be slain for thee –
> Though that I know before that I should die.

This seems to be exactly what Everyman wants, but risking a thoughtless death in the intensity of action is one thing; the long, arduous, spiritual pilgrimage facing the *fact* of death, and all the exacting moral demands implied by this, is quite another, and when Fellowship learns what Everyman is really up to he begins to slide out:

> That is matter indeed! Promise is duty,
> But, and I should take such a voyage on me,
> I know it well, it should be to my pain:
> And it makes me afeard, certain.
> But let us take counsel here as well as we can,
> For your words would fear a strong man.

Pressed, he refuses peremptorily, and makes his escape. Fellowship, the ordinary, as distinct from every man, will not face the spiritual realities which destroy life's easy pleasures.

Kindred and Cousin, briefer but not less seemingly wholehearted in their professions of loyalty, are curter in their refusals, Cousin making a token excuse insulting in its ludicrous lameness:

> No, by our Lady; I have the cramp in my toe.

All three false friends make use of religious expressions: Fellowship wishes Everyman 'God speed on thy journey'; Kindred swears by Saint Anne, and Cousin by the Virgin; they recognise the letter of religion, but use it only as a screen against the spirit.

The 'unworldly' personages have less character than the worldly ones; this, however, does not arise from artistic failure on the author's part, but from his putting them to a different use. He is concerned in the second half of the play to show how Everyman can be regenerated, under what influences, and what is the true purpose of the assets he will then possess. At first his only asset is Good-deeds, and Good-deeds is helpless. This is the nadir of Everyman's desperation – but a nadir may also be a turning-point. Good-deeds recommends to him the help of Knowledge, and, spontaneously Knowledge appears. She is the first and only figure to appear spontaneously of all those on whom Everyman relies, for she is really Faith and a free gift of God; but she can and will appear only when Everyman is fit to receive her. He is now fit, for his very desperation is itself a kind of knowledge – a recognition of the fact of his own helplessness. Only when he has seen the untruth of all that he has hitherto taken for knowledge is he able to understand and use the Knowledge that has real meaning.

In effect, Knowledge uses him, for she changes everything: Everyman is able to undergo the ministrations of Confession and is absolved; Good-deeds is thereby freed, and Everyman is enabled to summon to his aid his qualities of Discretion, Strength, Five-wits, and Beauty – all of which he must already have possessed, but none as yet rightly understood and employed.

The introduction of these qualities makes clear the real nature of the crisis which Everyman has been facing. When Death appears to him early on, it is natural to suppose that Everyman's life is already on the point of ending; but if this were so, what would be the use to him of Beauty and her colleagues? One realises now that Everyman is in robust mid-career, in no imminent danger of death, so far as he or anyone else can discern. But as with many another man in middle life, the reality of death suddenly impresses itself upon his imagination; he awakens to it, as that which is awaiting him not in the distant future, but perhaps round the next corner: 'For suddenly I do come.' In the light of this awakening, he assesses his life for the first time, with the result that he awakens not merely to the reality of Death, but to Truth itself. In this Truth, we are to suppose, he leads out the remainder of his days, all his natural self now dedicated to his supernatural goal. When he nears it, his new friends in turn abandon him. They go in due order; first, Beauty; next, Strength; then, Discretion; after him, Five-wits. For this is a real man dying, and such is the process of the gradual relinquishment of life. At the grave door, even Knowledge leaves him, for Knowledge *of* the Supreme Reality is useless to him at the moment in which he is to face that Reality itself. Only Good-deeds can go into the grave with him. Thus there is no mitigation for Everyman of his death; the austere dignity of his final speech accords with the awesome loneliness of dying:

> Into thy hands, Lord, my soul I commend;
> Receive it, Lord, that it be not lost;
> As thou me boughtest, so me defend,
> And save me from the fiend's boast,
> That I may appear with that blessed host
> That I shall be saved at the day of doom.
> *In manus tuas* – of might's most
> For ever – *commendo spiritum meum.*

Character creation of a rich, extended kind seems an impossibility in such a play. All the characters, except God, are figurative or representative, so that each can be shown only in a single aspect or in generalisation. Some of the characters are properties of Everyman himself; some, such as Goods, Fellowship, Cousin and Kindred, have a kind of independence, but no interest which is not bound up with interest in him. Others – notably Knowledge – have a spiritual identity but are factors in the plot rather than characters in it. Everyman himself must, by definition, dispense with any great particularity.

However, such comments evade the truth of the work. A real life is lived before us; a real death is died; Everyman is real man. How is this done? First, the writer's imaginative vision of human experience is psychologically valid still. From the moment that Death stops him in his tracks – 'Everyman, stand still' – through all his vicissitudes to the very last, we watch a human being undergoing the bitter process of self-realisation. He suffers loss of value in all he has valued to the point of despair; he achieves recovery, not of self-sufficiency, yet attaining for the first time to integrity; as death approaches he suffers loss again, and a more terrible loss, for his Beauty, Strength, Discretion and Five-wits are intimately his as Goods and Fellowship could never be, however much prized. Thanks to Knowledge, this second abandonment causes him no despair, but it still causes him grief and great fear. When at last he meets Death's summons, he has nothing but his faith, humility, memory of good deeds, and the dignity in the face of reality which they afford him. One may almost say that he *is* nothing, but this would not be true; he is a man who is dying.

Secondly, the author's treatment of Everyman's attributes gives one an authentic sense of the structure of a personality. We see how at first Everyman binds himself to extrinsic people and things; at the beginning of the play he is dependent on what is outside himself, and takes his colour from them. Later, when he achieves an intrinsic reality, his faith, faculties, and aspects are still shown to be his only by God's grace. All that Everyman at any time really owns, the only attribute that is inalienable, is Good-deeds. This austere view of human personality is not tenable only in terms of a Christian metaphysics; Everyman's good deeds are his impact on the world, and what other reality, in the long run, could he have?

None the less, such a metaphysic is what made possible such an image. Greater variety and immediacy in characterisation lay in the future, with comparable depth, but not profundity achieved with such simple means.

2. SIR GAWAYN AND THE GREEN KNIGHT

For the medieval, humanity revealed its nature through imaginative literature in different ways under different forms of treatment. *Everyman*, with its spiritual, didactic purpose, is cast in the allegorical form; *Sir Gawayn and the Green Knight* – a romance, its didacticism only implicit – is in the symbolic. The differences between the two forms are great, but the only one that need concern us at the moment is that whereas in the play each character lacks meaning in itself but, so to speak, signposts itself towards a nucleus of meaning, in the romance the characters demand acceptance for themselves, and though they have an ulterior meaning which arises out of the whole poem, this does not dissolve or efface their immediate impact.

With one all-important exception, the characters are not highly particularised; yet they are presented with force. People are never presented without being vitally present. This is true even of the unidentifiable lords and ladies of the Court scenes; they are never as though merely painted on back-cloths.

Wyle New Yer was so yep[1] . that hit was newe cummen,
That day doubble on the dais . was the douth[2] served,
Fro the king was cummen . with knightes into the halle,
The chauntre of the chapel . cheved[3] to an ende.
Loude crye was ther kest . of clerkes and other,
Noel nayted[4] onewe, . nevened[5] ful ofte;
And sithen riche[6] forth runnen . to reche hondeselle[7],
Yeayed[8] year-giftes on high . yelde hem bi hond,
Debated busily . about tho giftes;
Ladies laghed ful loude, . thogh thay lost haden,
And he that wan was not wrothe, . that may ye wel trawe.

It is the spirit of the King's youthfulness that permeates this
young Court; he is almost youth personified – but not idealised.
There is a touch of causticity in the description:

He was so joly of his joyfnes, . and wumwhat childgered[9]:
His lif liked hym light, . he lovied the lasse
Auther to longe lye . or to longe sitte,
So busied him his yonge blod . and his brain wylde.

The focus of the scene, as the Court take their places and
stand waiting for dinner to begin, is the Queen; like everyone
else, she is 'ful gay', but only the silk bedecked chair in which
she sits and the gem-starred canopy above her head are
described, not her person. The life of the Court centres on her,
but more as a symbol than as a person. Woman arouses
passions, but exacts their control through the exercises of
chivalry, courtesy and modesty by men, who must also sub-
limate these passions through the spirit of high adventure.
These are the qualities extolled by the Arthurian order of
civilisation, and they are crowned and guaranteed by the
virtue of good faith, the irrefragibility of the pledged word. So
Guinevere sits in an aura of rich fabrics and blazing gems,
because she is representatively the magnet of virile ardour and
a lofty code.

But men and their aspirations are not one; throughout the
poem there is tension between the frailty of the flesh and the

[1] sharp. [2] company. [3] came. [4] celebrated. [5] named.
[6] courtiers. [7] gifts. [8] proclaimed. [9] somewhat boyish.

variety and intensity of the assaults upon it. It is Sir Gawayn who is the self-chosen sample for this assault, and a fitting one, since he is held to be the exemplar in the court of all the knightly virtues. Just how much, under stress, is the proclamation of these virtues worth? It is this which Gawayn has to prove, though the full extent of the ordeal is only apparent to him at their very end, when he finds to his disgust that, by his own exalted standards, though not in the opinion of his peers and his King, he has failed. He has to keep faith by honouring an appointment, though his fate in doing so seems to be certain death; he must endure exposure to a bitter winter in mountain country, with no protection but his armour; he must fight with ogres and monsters. But none of this is unexpected to him. What takes him by surprise and nearly defeats him is that he has to resist the seductive advances of his host's beautiful young wife without either betraying her or showing her the least discourtesy. He is thus subjected to test in all the Arthurian virtues successively, and is somewhat in the role of an Everyman of aristocracy. Like Everyman, his personality seems at first colourless but is real, and reveals itself cumulatively.

Initially, Gawayn's personality has a colour and force which derives from the vividness with which the poet endows the court as a whole; and that vividness is not merely a quality of youthful gaiety, but of a heightened mood, a pitch of expectancy connected with the festival itself. 'The New Yer was so yep' – sharp – and the nerves are keen. It is a time of darkness and death – mid-winter – but also a time of beginnings. Arthur will not himself sit down to eat until he has heard or seen some new marvel, and again we have that expressive, forgotten syllable:

> Therefore of face so fere[1]
> He stightles[2] stif in stalle,
>   Ful yep in that New Yere
> Much mirthe he was with alle.

The Court with its gaiety and opulence is a challenge to the darkness and cold, as its values of life and order are a challenge

[1] proud. [2] stands motionless.

to death and disorder. In what particular substantial form will the challenge be met?

The answer comes with the most remarkable character in the tale – the Green Knight on his green horse, who 'hales in' at the hall door. More than life-size and green even to the flesh, he is entirely a creature of magic, and weird too is the challenge he forthrightly issues: that any knight present shall give him a blow with the huge axe that he carries, on condition that the same knight shall repair to the Green Chapel for a return blow a year and a day thereafter. Yet there is nothing fey about the long, detailed description of his appearance – his garb, his horse and its harness, the holly branch that he carries. Nor are his behaviour and personality insubstantial, as he twists about on his saddle, glaring round with his 'rede eyen' at the silent, awe-stricken hall, awaiting his answer; and then, when none is forthcoming, breaks into lusty mockery of Arthur and his Court. Nor is his decapitation by Gawayn an insubstantial affair; Gawayn strikes so truly that the blade cuts into the ground, and the severed head is spurned away by the feet of the audience as it bounces about the floor. Yet the Green Knight blithely gets to his feet, picks up his head, mounts his horse, and telling Gawayn to keep the appointment at the Green Chapel, rides back into the night:

> Halled out at the hal dor, . his hed in his hande,
> That the fyr of the flint . flaghe fro fole hoves[1].

The identity of the Green Knight somewhat resembles that of the sculptor Henry Moore's figures in stone: as they are the fusion of a human body with a mountain landscape, so he is a fusion of a man and a tree, like a forest deity in an animistic religion. Nature, in all its vehemence, indestructibility and relentlessness, has entered Arthur's hall. We may seek to rise above nature and her turbulence through civilisation, but she pulls us down; the most we can expect is to achieve a relationship in tension with her, acknowledging her impulses, but riding them as the Green Knight rides his horse.

This is fabled in the second half of the poem, when Gawayn,

[1] flew from his horse's hooves.

after roaming dangerously in the wintry mountains, comes to
the castle of Sir Bercilak de Hautdesert, becomes his guest, and
endures the advances of his seductive wife. He may not yield
to these advances, for this would be to betray his host; but he
must not rebuff them outright, for this would violate the rule
of courtesy. Moreover, as a knight, he must not appear
ridiculous to the lady, and he is somewhat ridiculously placed;
he is in bed when the lady visits him, and she makes three visits
on successive days. Each day, Sir Bercilak himself goes out
hunting, and he complicates Gawayn's position further by
stipulating that in return for a gift from himself of game,
Gawayn must pass on to him whatever he himself has received.
Now the lady gives him kisses, and these he duly conveys to
Bercilak, without, of course, naming the donor: one kiss on the
first day; two on the second; three on the third. But on the third
day, the lady also gives him a girdle which will protect him
against bloodshed. This Gawayn gratefully accepts – he will
need it in his encounter with the Green Knight – but he conceals it from her husband for fear of compromising her. To this
small extent he fails the ordeal; the dilemma is too hard for him.

Meanwhile Sir Bercilak has been bringing home to him the
spoil of his hunt, and each beast is emblematic of one of the
human vices to which Gawayn is in danger of giving way; a
deer, representing cowardice, a boar for brutishness, and a fox
for cunning. Sir Bercilak is in fact the Green Knight himself in
normal human form and contrasted guise, though with the
same personality and physique:

> A huge hathe[1] for the nones[2], . and of highe elde[3],
> Brode, bright, was his berde, . and al bever-hewed[4],
> Sturne[5], stif on the strithe[6] . on stalworth shonkes,
> Felle[7] face as the fyr, . and fre of his speche;
> And wel him semed, for sothe, . as the segge[8] thught,
> To lede a lordship in lee[9] . of leudes[10] ful gode.

He is now 'presentable' and would startle no one at King
Arthur's or any other court; he is a knight of flesh and blood as

---

[1] knight. [2] indeed. [3] advanced age. [4] reddish brown. [5] grim.
[6] standing firm. [7] grim. [8] knight (Gawayn). [9] peace and security.
[10] people.

Gawayn is. Yet he is serving still a third role: he is the hunter. Where once he was green but for his fiery eyes, now he is all fiery, the hue expressive of his fierceness. The prolonged exuberance of the graphic hunting scenes contrast with the secret stillness of Gawayn's bedroom where the lady carries on her colloquies, but Gawayn is Bercilak's prey, as much as the boar, the deer and the fox, and the emblematic nature of these beasts make the connection closer.

Once again the Green Knight in the final episode at 'the Green Chapel', which is not really a chapel but a cave in the rocks, Sir Bercilak shows the same ogreish humour that he has displayed from the start. In accordance with the pact, he makes a pass at Gawayn with his axe, and then pauses to mock at him for flinching. He makes a second pass, and pauses, to Gawayn's indignation, to jeer some more; on the third stroke, Bercilak just grazes Gawayn's neck. The first two passes which left Gawayn unscathed, were for the first two days at the castle, when Gawayn evaded the lady and kept faith with his host; the third stroke which just drew blood, was for the third day, when Gawayn failed in his pledge to the extent of suppressing the gift of the green girdle. Sir Bercilak then explains that he and the Green Knight are the same. He goes on to explain the mystery. An old lady in the castle, whom the poet has described at length, is really Morgan the Fay, the enchantress half-sister of Arthur and his great enemy. It is her magic that has contrived the whole adventure, with the aim of humiliating Arthur's Court and killing one of his best knights.

Morgan is introduced to Gawayn together with Bercilak's lady –

> Bot unlike on to loke . tho ladies were,
> For if the yonge was yep[1], . yolwe[2] was that other;

– so her age, ugliness and wintry malice contrasts with the youth, beauty, vitality, not only of the young lady but of Arthur's Court and its ardent ideals. Youth decays into age, as spring into winter. Ideals should not decay; yet what sustains them? Arthurian ideals need Arthurian civilisation; yet the

[1] fresh. [2] yellow, withered.

refinement of that civilisation may sap the virility of its ideals. Hence, they also need the ardour of Arthurian youth; yet that same ardour may laze into brutish lust. So civilisation – the Arthurian style of medieval civilisation at its best – must at once be nourished by nature, and yet always outfacing nature's challenge, as Gawayn endures his winter journey through the mountains, keeps faith with Sir Bercilak in both his guises, and refuses the lady without rebuffing her.

3. DESTINY AND ENVIRONMENT

In the play and the romance, medieval man faces his destiny and his environment respectively; the one, life-affirming though it is, shows how death should direct the conduct of life in this world, and the other shows on what terms life in this world offers its own fulfilment. Both works display complete assurance: the issue in each may be in doubt, but there is no doubt about what are the contending forces. Behind *Everyman* stands the power and all-pervasiveness of the Church and its teaching; behind *Gawayn and the Green Knight* stand the secular powers with their social codes and the immanence of an unsubdued nature.

Because they do not question the terms and aims of human life, the authors give to their works a ritual action. The fictions are formalised, not because the authors are abstract in their vision, but because for them living is enacted by given forces with known operations. For us, who feel destiny, environment and the operations of human nature itself to be uncertain factors, fictions become explorations, and the characters have to be defined or to achieve definition if we are to understand what sort of exploration is being expressed. For medieval man, character was pre-defined by the nature of the world and its Creator; fictions were demonstrations of roles. It is as though we were watching a great game of chess, in which each piece has his specific moves: King, Knight, or Pawn; Macbeth, Gawayn, or Everyman. The prescribed moves will tell us half what we need to know of the character, and the rest depends on the quality of the piece in question, for the game, as in *Alice Through the Looking-Glass*, is played by the pieces themselves.

The advantage of this vision of human nature is this: the vitality of the characters at their best is fed into them from great reservoirs of meaning beyond themselves – reservoirs we may label Nature, God, Carnal Love, or Evil, but which are felt to be substantial, not abstract. Variety, psychological minuteness, above all the sense of growth and continuous transition – these may be absent or relatively scarce, but in exchange we have in abundance the experience of personality. A modern fiction often resembles a piece of timber with numerous hard knots – the characters – but little continuous grain; medieval fictions such as these have strong flowing grain – the whole content of the poem – and few knots. Thus it is commonly hard to discuss the characters of a medieval tale without discussing everything; in a modern tale, it is often tempting and easy to isolate the characters. The great exception – the writer of the Middle Ages in whom modern and medieval most seem to meet – is, of course, Geoffrey Chaucer.

Chapter 2

Women by Chaucer
THE WIFE OF BATH · CRISEYDE

I. THE PILGRIMS

In medieval art, variety seems often meant to be an end in itself, yet again and again the end of this variety turns out to be coherence. The *Canterbury Tales* is a most medieval poem: the tales are not a mere medley, and the Pilgrims, though a fortuitous concourse, are not a haphazard collection. In the tales, piety, fable, romance and raw comedy compose into an image in which religious ideals of perfect virtue (the Clerk's Tale) are set beside earthly romances of exalted feeling (the Knight's Tale), and both are counterbalanced by discerning satire on the one hand – the Nun's Priest's Tale – and sensual comedy of the human animal – the Miller's Tale – on the other. The resulting image of human reality, compounded of higher aspirations and lower fulfilments, acknowledgement of spiritual truths together with submission to fleshy facts, would not cohere if the tales stood without tellers. The tales are the fictional exempla of experience to which the tellers add a dimension as real life exempla; the former cast reflections upon the latter, and the latter comment upon the former and upon one another. Not only do we have several modes of tale, not only are the tellers there to give a varied illusion of actuality to back and mingle with their tales, but Chaucer displays the medieval propensity to modulate in any one tale between the symbolic and the actual, a gift distinctive of an age for which to see and to understand was to allegorise and to symbolise. What at one moment seems fanciful and abstract may suddenly become concrete and everyday; or the typically life-size may enlarge itself to representation of great forces. One needs such considerations in mind when one contemplates such a figure as the Wife of Bath.

2. THE WIFE OF BATH

And so bifel that ones, in a Lente,
(So ofte tymes I to my gossib wente,
For ever yet I lovede to be gay,
And for to walke, in March, Averille, and May,
Fro hous to hous, to here sondry talis),
That Jankin clerk, and my gossib dame Alis,
And I my-self, in-to the feldes wente.
Myn housbond was at London al that Lente;
I hadde the bettre leyser for to pleye,
And for to see, and eek for to be seye
Of lusty folk; what wiste I wher my grace
Was shapen for to be, or in what place?
Therefore I made my visitaciouns,
To vigilies and to processiouns,
To preching eek and to thise pilgrimages,
To pleyes of miracles and mariages,
And wered upon my gaye scarlet gytes[1].
Thise wormes, ne thise motthes, ne thise mytes,
Upon my peril, frete hem never a deel;
And wostow why? for they were used weel.
Now wol I tellen forth what happed me.
I seye, that in the feldes walked we,
Til trewely we hadde swich daliance,
This clerk and I, that of my purveyance[2]
I spak to him, and seyde him, how that he,
If I were widwe, sholde wedde me.
For certeinly, I sey for no bobance[3],
Yet was I never with-outen purveyance
Of mariage, n'of othere thinges eek.
I holde a mouses herte nat worth a leek,
That hath but oon hole for to sterte to,
And if that faille, thanne is al y-do.
I bar him on honde,[4] he hadde enchanted me;
My dame taughte me that soutiltee.
And eek I seyde, I mette[5] of him al night;
He wolde han slayn me as I lay up-right,
And al my bed was ful of verray blood,
But yet I hope that he shal do me good;

¹ dresses. ² foresight. ³ boast. ⁴ made him believe. ⁵ dreamed.

For blood bitokeneth gold, as me was taught.
And al was false, I dremed of it right naught,
But as I folwed ay my dames lore,
As wel of this as of othere thinges more.
But now sir, lat me see, what I shal seyn?
A! ha! by god, I have my tale ageyn.

Her essence lies as much in these lines as anywhere. We see in
them much of her attitude to husbands, to clothes, to the world,
to religion, to herself. She is wooing her fifth husband before
the death of her fourth, who was none the less her favourite
though he took a mistress, for she much preferred the last two
husbands, who were bad, to the first three who were good. The
clue to this perversity seems to be astrological:

For certes, I am al Venerien
In felinge, and myn herte is Marcien.
Venus me yaf my lust, my likerousnesse,
And Mars yaf me my sturdy hardinesse.

Love of the grossest, most fleshly sort was her main pursuit, but
it must involve conflict: so much the better, if her husbands
offered her a fight. Alisoun is in everything physical and utterly
self-preoccupied. There is no life but her life, and that is gratification of her senses. The virtues which she in consequence
esteems are curious parodies of those enjoined by the Church;
her 'purveyance', for example, is a kind of prudence, but a
prudence which will dally with mortal sin. Yet she is not, by
her lights, being false to her fourth husband; the seduction of a
potential fifth is merely something which she owes to herself.
Thus she also has a great esteem for patience and humility, but
they are virtues for the husband to display, by a kind of natural
law. His doing so first, will enable her to follow, as in this sample
discourse to one of her first three:

Ye sholde been al pacient and meke,
And han a swete spyced conscience,
Sith ye so preche of Jobes pacience.
Suffreth alwey, sin ye so wel can preche;
And but ye do, certein we shal yow teche

43

> That it is fair to have a wyf in pees.
> Oon of us two moste bowen, doutelees;
> And sith a man is more resonable
> Than womman is, ye moste been suffrable.

She even has a kind of constancy, for a few lines further on, she points out that she could do very well for herself as a prostitute, but she makes a virtue of keeping her charms for him. She knew how to make her fourth husband jealous in revenge for his mistress, but insists that she did not actually commit adultery. And there is no reason to suspect her of lying; her public reputation is important to her – she cannot bear, we are told in the main Prologue, to have another woman take precedence of her in church. Besides the motive of not ruining herself by a scandal, it seems that her own peculiar brand of faithfulness is instigated by yet another parody of virtue: she is completely devoted, if not exactly to her husbands, then to the marital relationship as she interprets it – to the goal of a complete mastery.

The chief of the virtues that she parodies is of course that of piety. She is addicted to pilgrimages, which is why she is on this one. They serve as a sort of spiritual insurance, as well as providing opportunities for the sort of pleasures that she enjoys. Thus in her there is yet another parody of doctrine: instead of the body serving the soul, the spiritual is incarnated in the worldly:

> . . . what wiste I wher my grace
> Was shapen for to be, or in what place?
> Therefore I made my visitaciouns
> To vigilies . . .
>
> . . . . .
>
> And wered upon my gaye scarlet gytes.

What sort of grace does she seek? She attends religious occasions, but in her best clothes, to see and be seen. The sacred overtone of 'grace' is sunk into the sense of 'gratification'.

> Thise wormes, ne thise motthes, ne thise mytes,
> Upon my peril, frete[1] hem never a deel;
> And wostow why? for they were used weel.

[1] consumed them not at all.

'Lay not up for yourselves treasures upon earth where the moth and rust doth corrupt.' Her clothes are her treasures, and she doesn't 'lay them up' anywhere, not even in a chest: she keeps the moth away by constant use. And it was Lent when she went walking in the fields to catch her fifth husband – the season of abstinence. But again, Lent falls in the spring, the season of mating and generation.

If the Wife sees no difficulty in reconciling the demands of the Church with those of Nature, this is not because she is in a state of unconscious confusion. In the course of the first 160 lines of her Prologue, she faces the dilemma boldly. 'Virginitee is greet perfeccioun' she acknowledges, but on the other hand,

> Telle me also, to what conclousioun
> Were membres maad of generacioun,
> And for what profit was a wight y-wroght?

There are those who follow the rule of virginity, and they are like bread of 'pured whete-seed'; there are others, like herself, who may be called barley-bread

> And yet with barley-breed, Mark telle can,
> Our Lord Jesu refresshed many a man.

So far she is on safe ground. The real case against her is that she is not a refresher of men; she is their destroyer, though they desire her. Blake saw her in these terms:

The lady prioress, in some ages, predominates; and in some the wife of Bath, in whose character Chaucer has been equally minute and exact, because she is also a scourge and a blight. I shall say no more of her, nor expose what Chaucer has left hidden; let the young reader study what he has said of her: it is useful as a scarecrow. There are of such characters born too many for the peace of the world.

There is no difficulty in accepting Blake's verdict when one sets beside it the Wife's own pronouncement:

> An housbonde I wil have, I nil not lette,
> Which shal be bothe my dettour and my thral,
> And have his tribulacioun withal
> Up-on his flessh, whyl that I am his wyf.

And here one may most usefully return to the astrological interpretation of her character, expounded by W. 'C. Curry in *Chaucer and the Medieval Sciences*. It was widely held that at birth people received their constitution in accordance with the position of the stars and planets, and that these and Fortune governed their lives in so far as they lived them on merely a physical plane. Only piety – not the Wife's sort – and Divine Grace could raise a man above his temperament and chance, for these were all that governed existence 'under the Moon'. The Wife's lechery and aggressiveness derive from the predominance of Mars and Venus at her birth, and since her temperament is also her chosen way of life, she lives by them.

One penalty she must pay is to face the onset of age, which, often together with the figure of Death, hovers in personification over 'lusty folk' in medieval fictions. So she half personifies her own ageing in the only sad, bitter lines in her Prologue:

> Unto this day it dooth myn herte bote[1]
> That I have had my world as in my tyme.
> But age, allas! that al wol envenyme,
> Hath me biraft my beauty and my pith;
> Lat go, farewel, the devel go therwith!
> The flour is goon, ther is na-more to telle,
> The bren,[2] as I best can, now moste I selle;
> But yet to be right mery wol I finde.

The recovery, it can be seen, is none the less swift. Her way of life has optimism inseparable from it; it is part of the aggressiveness of her temperament.

Another penalty she only risks: that she may meet her match. The Wife's Prologue seems to sprawl shapelessly, but it has form. So far as the plot is concerned – for the Prologue is just as much a tale as any of the tales – the ageing of the Wife is counterpointed by the increasing youthfulness of her husbands. The first three were older than herself; men who above all wanted peace in their homes and were therefore destined to give way to her in the end. The fourth seems to have been nearer her own age and hunted elsewhere. The fifth was younger

[1] good. [2] bran.

and confronted her with an aggressiveness equal to her own. He endures no long diatribes as the first three husbands did, but administers them instead; moreover he reads them out of books to give them full weight of established authority. For a change, we think of her as a much-provoked woman when at last she snatches three pages from his favourite work and throws them on the fire. He strikes her down, but, on the verge of defeat at last, she yet triumphs over him too. In penitence and fear, he submits himself and his goods to her entirely. In return, she makes him a model wife. But one is left with the sense that the Wife is foredoomed to tragedy, for a husband she must have, and evidently, the older she grows, the younger and the more spirited must he be. Sooner or later, then, she must face a double subjection: to her age, and to a spouse; and she has no resources in her character with which to endure it.

So ends the Wife's Prologue. Research has suggested that it is in its form itself a parody of the correct scholarly way of presenting a case – an Apology, in fact. The Wife has also completely exposed her personality after the medieval convention of the 'confession' – the Pardoner's Prologue is another example – and the exposure is in its way a most eloquent defence. She has bodied herself forth in the words, much as a dancer bodies forth a dance through movement. The words, indeed, are movement, rhythmical as dance, as sensuous and as varied in tempo. The effect is an abundant manifestation of life in one of its most powerful aspects. To say that the Wife is self-centred is inadequate, for the word suggests an inert, Euclidean kind of figure and ignores her quality of momentum, of outpouring. The Wife may be a destructive force, but she is also an enriching one, and though she is her own main object of enrichment, so is she her own ultimate victim.

Her Tale is about half as long as her Prologue, and, coming after it, is unexpected in its style. It is a courtly romance, suavely delivered, but it has the same upshot – that woman's 'moste desyr' is 'to have sovereyntee'. It re-tells the theme of the Prologue, but in romance terms. Life is not like that – not merely because the woman in the Tale is an enchantress, capable of transforming herself from a hag into an entrancing beauty, but because in life people do not submit to each other with this graciousness. What life might be is romance – is gracious and mellow; but in reality it is raw and violent, and harmony between equals is often achieved only after a fight by the fireside.

C. S. Lewis in *The Allegory of Love* says of the late Latin writers that they inaugurated the world of myth and fancy for the poet, so that henceforth he could enter three realms in all: the daily one, or the world of the probable; that enshrining his religion, or 'the marvellous taken as fact'; and that of 'the marvellous known to be fiction'. So Chaucer proceeds in the *Canterbury Tales*, and so he presents the Wife of Bath. We see her in sensual fact, speaking of her own experience; we see her against her religion, to which she is in one perspective so close and from which in another she is sundered so far; and we see her contrasted with her own fiction, where the passions operate to fulfilment, without squalor or violence.

3. CRISEYDE

Our first glimpse of her is in the temple, where Troilus, son of King Priam, also sees her for the first time, and is completely conquered.

> Among thise othere folk was Criseyde
> In widewe's habite blak; but nathelees,
> Right as our firste lettre is now an A[1],
> In beautee first so stood she, makelees[2];
> Hir godly looking gladede al the prees[3].
> Has never seyn thing to ben preysed derre
> Nor under cloude blak so bright a sterre
>
> As was Criseyde, as folk seyd everichoon
> That hir behelden in hir blake wede[4];
> And yet she stood ful lowe and stille alloon
> Behinden othere folk in liter brede[5],
> And neigh the dore, ay under shames drede,
> Simple of a-tyr, and debonaire of chere,
> With ful assured loking and manere.

[1] An allusion to Anne, Queen of Richard II.   [2] matchless.   [3] crowd.
[4] dress.   [5] in a small space.

She is a widow, but very young, and black offsets beauty; yet her weeds hang about her like a cloud. A mere token, considered as mourning, they are formidable as an omen. Because of her beauty, she is conspicuous, but she stands retired, seeking to evade attention, 'ay under shames drede'. There are several reasons for this attitude of withdrawal. She is a young widow and easily compromised; more important, her father, Calchas, has betrayed her as he has betrayed the Trojans by deserting to the Greeks, for he is a seer who has foreseen the downfall of Troy. Her own status in the city, therefore, is heavily compromised. Yet she is debonnaire in her bearing and assured in her looks and behaviour: her menacing circumstances do not daunt her, do not really touch her. Perhaps her deliberate withdrawal from attention is a half-conscious seeking of it; like the Wife of Bath, is she seeking the best of both worlds? But unlike the Wife, she displays breeding in all her appearance and behaviour; an aristocrat, therefore, her right setting is a Court, and her right lover, a Prince.

When she becomes conscious of Prince Troilus' prolonged stare, she casts an arch glance towards him and brightens up:

> . . . for she let falle
> Hir loke alite a-side, in swich manere,
> Ascaunces, 'what! may I not stonden here?'
> And after that hir loking gan she lighte,
> That never thoughte him seen so good a sighte.

So it is that she makes the first move in their relationship, but to what extent does she know she has made it? On the one hand, she is far from wanting the entanglements of a love affair; on the other, the lightening of her looks is certainly pleasure that her loveliness has found its mark.

Criseyde is as elusive as the Wife is unmistakable, and the heart of her enigma is contained by the phrase 'as false as Criseyde'. She and Troilus become lovers and their love is whole, passionate, ideal. Yet when, in an exchange of prisoners, she is later sent to the Greeks (on the demand of her father) in return for the Trojan Antenor, she is to give herself to the Greek Diomed, and this in contradiction to her parting pledge that she will steal back to Troy and to Troilus' arms. The story, of course, is not Chaucer's; he took it from Boccaccio, who took it from others, right back to the Romans who may have got it from the Greeks, though it does not occur in Homer. But the Criseyde of the legend is a girl who betrayed her lover, an anybody or a nobody according to treatment. It is Chaucer's Criseyde who is a person, who stands out of the narrative so that it is tempting to talk of her as though she existed apart from it – a temptation to be resisted at all costs, but a main sign of a vivid creation. To dress a classical legend as a courtly romance – this any medieval poet might have done and many did. It is Chaucer's individual achievement to fuse both with actuality – the marvellous-known-to-be-fiction with the world of the probable. It is Criseyde, Pandar, and to a less extent Diomed who stand out with this substance; Troilus, as though to remind the reader of that order of fiction whose unreality is being exposed, remains half a figure of ideal romance.

Because Criseyde is real, then, her betrayal of Troilus matters. Critics study her psychology microscopically to understand her motivation. What sort of statement is Chaucer making – about Criseyde, about woman, about love, about romance? Since such a creation is bound to remain an immemorial symbol, it is as well to know what sort of symbol we have on our hands. Other critics say these are mistaken. Chaucer was a medieval writer, and medieval writers were more interested in the action of a story than in psychological motivation, which, in our terms, they could in any case scarcely have understood. But then the action of the story should explain Criseyde's betrayal. Does it do so?

When we look at the action, we find that Criseyde is set in circle within circle of betrayal, and it is against these circumstances of treachery that she plights her eternal faith. On the outer circle, we have the fact that Troy is to fall by treachery, and the traitor is to be that very Antenor for whom Criseyde is to be exchanged. Her father deserts to the Greeks. Before Pandarus betrays her outright to Troilus, he and the Prince blackmail her into a half surrender: the young man is sick with desire – would she have his death on her head? To avert this,

she accepts him as her 'knight'. Then Pandarus admits Troilus
by a back way into his house where Criseyde is sheltering on a
stormy night. Pandarus, indeed, though he is shown as caring
for his niece, and as feeling responsible, in romantic terms, for
the permanence of the union, treats the task of capturing her as
an opportunity for the great game of hunting the lady – the
more so because he is unsuccessful in his own affairs – a cam-
paign, in which all stratagems are fair, and men have bonds with
one another transcending all but the romantic bonds with
women.

Yet the chief traitor is Criseyde's own nature – her nature, not
her 'self', if the distinction be allowed, for *she* is betrayed by her
own nature, as well as her lover. Chaucer is careful to stress the
femininity of this nature:

> . . . alle her limes so wel answeringe
> Weren to womanhode, that creature
> Was never the lesse mannish in seminge.

This is near the beginning of the poem. It is in the last book,
when she is faced with the choice between Troilus and Diomed,
that her qualities are summarised:

> She sobre was, eek simple, and wys withal,
> The beste y-norrished eek that mighte be,
> And goodly of hir speche in general,
> Charitable, estatliche[1], lusty and free
> Ne never-mo ne lakkede hir pitee;[2]
> Tendre-herted, slydinge of corage;[3] . . .

The listed qualities do not, themselves, express an individuality;
they make up a type. It is the type of aristocratically bred girl
inculcated with the qualities that specialise her, so to speak, for
court life: the kind of girl whose due is to be revered, guarded,
adored by noble young men, whose ardours she in turn will
assuage and refresh; the girl who, in that romantic allegory
(partly translated by Chaucer) *The Romaunt of the Rose*, is dis-
persed among symbols and allegorical figures, who is less a
person than, her status once compromised and its tethering
attachments shorn, a theatre for masculine adventures. While

[1] dignified. [2] she was never lacking in pity. [3] unstable in courage.

her affair with Troilus rests secure in its secrecy under his guardianship, she is all that the civilisation which produced her intended her to be – to the refinement and ennoblement of both herself and her lover. Once cast loose amongst the Greeks, without her lover and with even less status, she is merely a victim.

But the tale would lack the poignance and beauty that it possesses if Criseyde were merely a stereotype. Her qualities are ascribable to one, but she lives them out in three dimensions. On the one hand, she is the pretext for a game being played by Pandarus, and a stage for a romance in which she herself plays more than one part, even simultaneously; on the other, she is a person who moves out of one predicament into another, each brought about by others, in each of which she is rendered helpless either by circumstances or by her own disposition, and in each of which she more or less painfully suffers.

She is left in a predicament by her father's desertion, but Troilus' profession of love for her is a new one. When Pandarus breaks the news of it, she is first distressed and then confused; she runs to her room to think it out – 'And sette her down as stille as any stone' – and has just brought herself to the comfortable conclusion that the state of Troilus' heart need have no influence on her own, when a cry goes up in the house that the Prince and his men are about to pass down the street. She runs to the window, and watches him, the wounded hero, receiving the acclamations of the crowd with becoming bashfulness:

> For which he wex a litel reed for shame,
> Whan he the peple up-on him herde cryen,
> That to biholde it was a noble game,
> How sobreliche he caste down his een.
> Criseyde gan al his chere aspyen,
> And leet so softe it in her herte sinke,
> That to hir-self she syede, 'Who yaf me drinke?'

One realises that she has already been strongly attracted by the Prince, but now her impression of him sinks deep into her being, pours into her emotional depths, as an exquisitely refreshing drink transfigures the body to itself when one is thirsty. In the midst and in spite of the machinery of trickery, the setting of betrayal, the love of Troilus and Criseyde for each other is real, deep, and fulfilling. How then does she come to forsake him? In general terms we have explained it, but just as Chaucer makes us feel Criseyde's inner surrender to the Trojan, so, without indicating any change in her nature, he makes us feel her surrender to the Greek.

> This Diomede, as bokes us declare,
> Was in his nedes prest[1] and corageous;
> With sterne voys and mighty limes square,
> Hardy, testif[2], strong and chevalrous
> Of dedes, lyk his fader Tideus.
> And som men seyn, he was of tunge large . . .

Diomede is the coarse, bluff soldier in fact, a man who from the first, when he leads Criseyde away from Troy, sees in her an opportunity for a beguiling escapade. He sees the uselessness of a direct approach, however:

> For douteles, if she have in hir thought
> Him that I gesse, he may not been y-brought
> So sone awey; but I shal finde a mene,
> That she not wite as yet shal what I mene.

So he will use his own brand of cunning, and the cycle of predicaments begins again, and just as before, Criseyde's subtly conditioned nature is the most dangerous of the factors against her. This time, however, the predicaments are grimmer, and have no redeeming qualities. Again Criseyde is isolated, socially insecure, but her position in the Greek camp is more exposed than it had been in her own house in Troy. Again she is wooed by a prince, whom it would be even more dangerous to refuse, but he does not love her, and, with all Pandarus' cynicism, he is not only without her uncle's compensatory affection, but is quite ruthless. Her instinctive courtesy begins the process of her surrender by encouraging Diomede (the character of Belacoil – which might be translated 'Good Manners' – plays a similar role, as C. S. Lewis points out, in *The Romaunt of the Rose*), and

[1] prompt. [2] headstrong.

when she cannot bring herself to return to Troy as she has promised, she feels already that Troilus is half betrayed.

That she does not return is in keeping with all that she is: by breeding a focus for situations, she is not equipped to escape from them. Unlike the Wife of Bath with her 'purveyance', she is without initiative. Her civilisation – medieval civilisation, her classical setting notwithstanding – both made her and betrayed her, by building her up as all receptivity and responsiveness to its ideals, and then reducing her to the prey of its passions. But this, no doubt, is to put it rather anachronistically. Chaucer, of course, was not aware that he was writing of something we may call 'medieval civilisation'. His point is that betrayal is intrinsic to human nature, ever since Eve betrayed Adam, and Adam, God: 'Swich fyn hat false worldes brotelnesse.' On this earth, no faith can be put in human love, for as we live, so we betray those we love and our very selves. This accounts for Troilus' contemptuous laughter from the height of heaven, which critics have unaccountably found so painfully incongruous. Once again, but now in a very different way, Chaucer is applying his triple standard in the assessment of human values: that which man knows to be true in heaven, that which he would like to be true on earth, and that which he is. Or, paraphrasing, and inverting the order: that which Troilus and Criseyde are, that which they would like to be, and the bliss which can only be theirs in transience as earthly lovers.

4. THE WIFE AND CRISEYDE

The Wife by her carnality, Criseyde by her falsity, both widows are 'daughters of Eve' in a realer, more vivid sense than a modern writer could associate with the cant phrase. The Wife is all nature – purified, to speak paradoxically, of spirit; Criseyde is all yielding, the 'frailty that is woman'. Far as they seem, in pronounced ways, from each other, they have in common also the contradictoriness which men have associated with women. Each cherishes her independence, yet needs a man; each is capable of being false and true at the same time, without expecting men to understand; each is guileful by disposition, and not, like men, according to need; each is

54

capricious. Even in their widowhood, they have more in common than coincidence. A widow is on her own, yet not a virgin; she has been initiated, and accordingly is without the protection of innocence – the prophylactic against certain forms of temptation. The consequence of their status is to make the Wife more dangerous – the huntress watching for her victim – and Criseyde the more vulnerable – she shares knowledge with the men such as makes her more susceptible to their ploys.

Chaucer, it is possible to say, was, in these characters, with allowance made both for social differences and differences of formal mode – the romance, and the pseudo-realistic confession – creating two versions of Every-woman. The Everyman of the drama, though in form and expression distinctly male, was of course not sexually restricted; he comes to us in the end as 'every human', whereas Criseyde and Alisoun are female or nothing. Still, vastly more naturalistic as they seem, they are equally medieval in basic conception. Chaucer is drawing, that is to say, just as much on a great store of unitary conceptions, religious, moral, social, physical, according to which what human beings have in common is indisputably more meaningful than what they have distinguishingly; the former comprehends the human essence, and the latter only human accidents. This amounts to saying not only that Man is more important than men, which is a dictum we still pay lip-service to, but also that Man is more interesting, because more real.

Chapter 3

Kings

A STUDY OF *MACBETH*

I. THE THREE KINGS

THE play is set in the reign of the good King Duncan of Scotland, a contemporary of the saintly Edward the Confessor of England. Macbeth is a Scottish general who wins a complicated victory over Duncan's enemies, and is led on to murder Duncan and seize the throne himself. As Duncan was a just king, so the usurper becomes the type of a tyrant, a king with no scruples, frenzied with suspicion, unbounded in cruelty. The tragedy, though it would be misleading to describe it as a play about kingship, has a traditional view of the office as its axis, and the tradition is embodied in Duncan.

Duncan is usually ignored as a colourless character with a brief role, merely that of pretext for a murder. It is true that he speaks fewer than sixty lines, and disappears after the first act, and it is also true that in our way of looking at character he is insipid, a mere token of the 'good king and good man' who has vanished with the simplifications of forgotten nursery history books. Yet he is expressive of richness, that richness which Macbeth lays waste; he and the rebel Cawdor, who never appears on the stage, are the two keys to the play. If we do not use them we may be locked out from its mysteries.

In scene iv Duncan receives a report from his son, Malcolm, of Cawdor's execution. The traitor, whose title has passed to Macbeth, has died finely in full repentance, but he has been the King's confidant, and Duncan thus comments:

> There is no art
> To find the mind's construction in the face:
> He was a gentleman on whom I built
> An absolute trust.

At this point Macbeth enters – it is the first meeting between

56

him and the King since the battle – and Duncan turns to him with heartfelt welcome: 'O worthiest cousin!' There is no art, indeed, to find the mind's construction in the face, but Duncan does not lose his trust in human nature. Suspicion, as the play shows, is the seed of tyranny; Duncan is trusting because he is the opposite of a tyrant, and because he is generous.

Duncan goes on to express the most candid gratitude to Macbeth, whose services, says the King, have exceeded all scope of reward. To this Macbeth replies that it is the King's function to accept his subjects' duties which are, as such, their own reward. The reply is a proper one because the King is no mere man; in his person he is the state and more – the transmitter of divine sovereignty within the state. Duncan's answer is expressive:

> Welcome hither:
> I have begun to plant theee, and will labour
> To make thee full of growing.

He speaks like a forester – a forester of men, with the duty of raising the fortunes of his most deserving subjects. The image is carried on by Banquo, Macbeth's colleague in victory. Enfolded in Duncan's embrace he exclaims: 'There if I grow, the harvest is your own.'

Duncan's trustingness is evidence of his justice: a great cause of suspicion would be the resentment of wronged subjects. He combines majesty with humility: humility in the frankness of his gratitude, and majesty in his conception of the office he bears – stern towards treachery, generous in the nurturing and encouragement of virtue. Less a 'character' than a moral climate, yet a character in his immunity to meaner emotions, we find him rejoicing in the atmosphere that surrounds Macbeth's castle:

> This castle hath a pleasant seat; the air
> Nimbly and sweetly recommends itself
> Unto our gentle senses.

We know that his murder is being at this moment plotted within the castle – that again he is being horribly deceived. But he is also responding to the climate that is his own, that 'nimble' and 'sweet' air of God's nature, of Eden, at once pure and invigorating, which is the physical equivalent of the moral atmosphere that a just king affords his realm. A moment later we see him in his office as the mediator of divine worship and blessing in his remark on Lady Macbeth's demonstrative approach to welcome him:

> See, see, our honour'd hostess –
> The love that follows us sometime is our trouble
> Which still we thank as love. Herein I teach you,
> Now you shall bid God 'ild us for your pains,
> And thank us for your trouble.

Kings are often inconvenienced by the ostentatious devotions of their subjects but the devotion goes beyond the King to God, whose representative he is: God also rewards the King, as representative of the people.

So in scene vii Macbeth, contemplating his own crime as a public abomination, speaks of it thus:

> Besides, this Duncan
> Hath borne his faculties so meek, hath been
> So clear in his great office, that his virtues
> Will plead like angels, trumpet-tongued, against
> The deep damnation of his taking off. . . .

The eloquence of heaven itself speaks in the virtues of this just and beneficent king. More remarkable still is the language with which, after Duncan's murder, Macbeth seeks to explain away to the guests in his castle his killing of the grooms who guard the King's chamber:

> Here lay Duncan
> His silver skin lac'd with his golden blood;
> And his gash'd stabs look'd like a breach in nature
> For ruin's wasteful entrance: there, the murderers,
> Steep'd in the colours of their trade, their daggers
> Unmannerly breech'd with gore. . . .

That Macbeth is lying – the grooms are not murderers – is less important than the kind of truth that he is telling. A man's blood is not golden, and Duncan was a man; but by the office

58

he held he was also more than a man, and his blood is as gold, that kingly metal. Furthermore, the death of this mediator of divine justice and munificence is a catastrophe in nature: ruin rushes in to lay waste the social order, and that is part of the natural order.

He speaks prophetically. Macbeth, the tyrant King, spreads about him injustice and misery. More especially, ridden by suspicion himself, he scatters the seeds of it in the hearts of his subjects and of all concerned with Scotland. Notably this is so with Malcolm, Duncan's son, who has fled to England. Since it is a well-known device of dictatorships to send decoys after dangerous refugees to beguile them back into the tyrant's power, so, when Macduff appears in London, Malcolm does not know whether to trust him. To test Macduff's good faith, Malcolm paints a portrait of himself as a potential tyrant as black as Macbeth himself, for if Macduff still wants him to return after such a confession, his deceitfulness will be manifest. Only when, as Malcolm's confession culminates, Macduff is filled with horror and despair, is the Prince satisfied with his trustworthiness.

It is here that the English doctor enters, speaks four lines on Edward the Confessor's miraculous cures, and goes out again. Wedged between the dialogue on royal vices and Ross's entry with his dramatic disclosure of the massacre of Macduff's entire family, the English doctor seems pointless. But he is not so, nor is the point merely that Shakespeare wanted to flatter James I who himself attempted such cures. The point is that Edward, like Duncan, was a king from whom goodness flowed spontaneously, whereas Macbeth had made himself a disseminator of evil. A few lines on, Ross is thus describing Scotland:

> the dead man's knell
> Is there scarce asked for who; and good men's lives
> Expire before the flowers in their caps,
> Dying or e'er they sicken.

2. THE MURDERER

Duncan, then, stands for the positives in the play; for that health, growth, freedom and light which Macbeth perverts, stunts, eliminates and darkens. We must now consider the other key – Cawdor.

As the play opens, Macbeth has won a double victory over the invading King of Norway and over the rebellious Macdonald. Cawdor is part of this coalition, but his activities are mysterious. Ross first refers to him in scene ii:

> Norway himself
> With terrible numbers
> Assisted by that most disloyal traitor
> The thane of Cawdor, began a dismal conflict . . .

but Ross does not say what form Cawdor's assistance has taken. It only appears later that he cannot himself have appeared on the battlefield. In the meantime, Duncan orders Cawdor's execution, and confers his title on Macbeth. Macbeth hears of this first from the witches in the next scene, when they hail him first as Thane of Glamis, next as Thane of Cawdor, and last as 'king hereafter'. The first title does not surprise him, for he knows that he has come into it by the order of nature, by inheritance. The last, in his opinion, 'stands not within the order of belief'. The second, however, perplexes him equally, for –

> the thane of Cawdor lives
> A prosperous gentleman . . .

from which it appears that he is entirely ignorant of Cawdor's part in the rebellion. So when, a little later, Angus appears with official confirmation of the title, Macbeth again protests:

> The thane of Cawdor lives: why do you dress me
> In borrowed robes?
> ANGUS: Who was the thane lives yet:
> But under heavy judgement bears that life
> Which he deserves to lose. Whether he was combin'd
> With those of Norway, or did line the rebel
> With hidden help and vantage, or that with both
> He labour'd in his country's wrack, I know not;
> But treasons capital, confess'd and proved
> Have overthrown him.

Thus the exact nature of Cawdor's activities remain unknown

to us; we learn only that they were the worse for his having been Duncan's trusted intimate. He had deceived 'his bosom interest'. It is important to notice however, first, that before his speedy execution he redeems himself by frank confession and 'deep repentance', without any hope of mercy; and second, that it is from the moment that Macbeth finds that the witches have thus far spoken true that the evil begins to stir in him. It is as though the evil were conveyed with the guilty title.

But the symbolism goes deeper. Macbeth has just won a triple victory against the King's enemies; one comes from without – the King of Norway; one, Macdonwald, is an open rebel from within the realm; and Cawdor is a secret rebel, and a participator in Duncan's 'bosom interest'. But Macbeth now has to undergo an assault on his own soul which he likens to the state –

> My thought, whose murder yet is but fantastical,
> Shakes so my single state of man, that function
> Is smother'd in surmise. . . .

In the struggle that ensues, he is once more to face three enemies, and once more, one assaults from without and two from within. The enemy from without is the witches. One of those from within is his wife, to whom he sends an account of his meeting with the witches, and whom he addresses as 'my dearest partner of greatness'; the other is again Cawdor – that is to say, himself.

Had any one of these assailants been absent, Macbeth would not have been overthrown. If the witches had not made their predictions, he would not have written his letter, and his wife would not have seen her course of action. Had she then not brought the influence of her secret knowledge of him to bear, his own ambition would have failed. Had it not been for the secret enemy within himself, neither his wife nor the witches could have prevailed.

To identify this secret enemy is by no means easy; we tell ourselves very little by calling it ambition. The first scene gives us some help, for there the witches make their sinister appointment with him 'upon the heath', and utter their slogan 'Fair is foul and foul is fair', which he unconsciously echoes in scene iii

– 'So foul and fair a day I have not seen'. We learn thus that
Macbeth is in his nature vulnerable to evil beyond the normal
extent: a cord in his heart vibrates to Satan before he encounters Satan's emissaries. He calls the day 'foul', thinking
only of the bad weather, not foreseeing his forthcoming spiritual
defeat; and he calls it fair because of his recent victory. This
takes us back to scene ii, and the Sergeant's descriptions, for
instance, of Macbeth:

> Disdaining fortune, with his brandish'd steel,
> Which smok'd with bloody execution,
> Like valour's minion
> Carv'd out his passage till he fac'd the slave;
> Which ne'er shook hands, nor bade farewell to him
> Till he unseam'd him from the nave to the chops,
> And fix'd his head upon our battlements.

and again, this time speaking of Macbeth and Banquo together:

> As cannons overcharg'd with double cracks
> So they
> Doubly redoubled strokes upon the foe:
> Except they meant to bathe in reeking wounds,
> Or memorize another Golgotha,
> I cannot tell. . . .

The lines, in words and rhythm, express tumultuous bloodshed, demoniac ferocity and bloodthirstiness. Where will the
impetus thus generated in the heat of a battle against superior
forces find an end? The fighting beast so roused cannot be
called to heel like a dog. The witches speak their baffling predictions, and the rational self, the king of Macbeth's nature, is
dismayed at the inner violence that then rocks him:

> This supernatural soliciting
> Cannot be ill, cannot be good; – if ill
> Why hath it given me earnest of success,
> Commencing in a truth? I am thane of Cawdor.
> If good, why do I yield to that suggestion
> Whose horrid image doth unfix my hair,
> And make my seated heart knock at my ribs,
> Against the use of nature?

It is so that Macbeth is divided against himself. The fighting beast in him is sub-rational; roused by the bloodshed of battle, it seizes on the 'image' of a further bloodshed, the murder of the King, from which the sensitive, half toppled reason in the man recoils in horror.

> Stars, hide your fires;
> Let not light see my black and deep desires. . . .

One thing only pacifies the rapacity of that baser self, but unfortunately it is also anodyne to the distress of his moral reason; this is his public honour and reputation:

> He hath honour'd me of late; and I have bought
> Golden opinions from all sorts of people,
> Which would be worn now in their newest gloss,
> Not cast aside so soon.

Thus he protests to his wife in scene vii. The reputation he prizes is external to him, like clothes, as of course a reputation naturally is; but this indicates several important things. The first is that it is not his conscience that is primarily revolted – not that inner self which must justify his actions in the light of nature and of God, and for which public opinion would be altogether secondary. Another is that he does not expect to keep the murder secret. A third, that at this juncture his inner self has not quite abandoned conscience; it is, so to speak, driven to the perimeter of his personality, but it is still fighting. A fourth is that its chief ally is no longer love of good or horror of evil, but fear – fear of converting public love and admiration into loathing.

To understand Macbeth's state of mind, we have to understand the great soliloquy with which scene vii opens. Macbeth has withdrawn from his banqueting hall, where the King is his guest, to fight out his inner conflict.

> If it were done – when 'tis done – then 'twere well
> It were done quickly: if th'assassination
> Could trammel up the consequence, and catch,
> With this surcease, success; that but this blow
> Might be the be-all and the end-all here,
> But here upon this bank and shoal of time,
> We'd jump the life to come.

So far, he is saying that the murder must be isolated from before and after. It must leave no clues, no consequences, to entangle it with the web of life. If it could be accomplished in this way, then judgement in the hereafter life may be ignored. Our first question is, how does Macbeth manage to discount Divine Judgement so easily? And the answer is to be found in the rhythm of the speech. Just as in scene ii the words of the Sergeant's speech, describing Macbeth in battle, almost clot with their impetuousness, hardly able to keep abreast with the headlong violence they are seeking to convey, so here, they crowd and accumulate hectically in keeping with the agitation of the speaker's mind. That agitation, the expression of a monster within him that in its urgency can take only the present as its scope, crowds out vistas of eternity or any conception belonging to them. He goes on:

> But in these cases
> We still have judgement here; that we but teach
> Bloody instructions, which, being taught, return
> To plague the inventor: this even-handed justice
> Commends the ingredients of our poison'd chalice
> To our own lips.

Unable to contemplate the crime coolly, to plan it calmly, he feels all the more that retribution in this world will follow surely. 'Still' has the sense of 'always': Macbeth can see the murder only as an instant act of violence, and violence rouses violence against it, just as his own violence in battle has projected into him – with help by suggestion from the witches – the image of further violence in murder. He now turns to the point of view of the judgement he may expect. How will the world see the crime? What sort of man would he be killing, and in what circumstances?

> He's here in double trust:
> First, as I am his kinsman and his subject,
> Strong both against the deed; then, as his host,
> Who should against his murderer shut the door,
> Not bear the knife myself. Besides this Duncan
> Hath borne his faculties so meek, hath been

64

> So clear in his great office, that his virtues
> Will plead like angels, trumpet-tongued, against
> The deep damnation of his taking-off;
> And pity, like a naked new-born babe,
> Striding the blast, or heaven's cherubin, hors'd
> Upon the sightless couriers of the air,
> Shall blow the horrid deed in every eye,
> That tears shall drown the wind, – I have no spur
> To prick the sides of my intent, but only
> Vaulting ambition, which o'erleaps itself,
> And falls on the other.

He is murdering his lord, his relative, his guest; more than all, he is murdering a king who is beyond reproach. From this point, the heavenly array of Divine Judgement and avenging angels, which Macbeth has been able to dismiss as appertaining to the next world, comes fully into support of the judgement that he expects in this, and not surprisingly when we recall, as Macbeth does, how Duncan has carried out his sacred functions. Yet still it is the judgement of men that Macbeth fears – 'Shall blow the horrid deed in every eye / That tears shall drown the wind'. Macbeth thus stands outside himself, and sees his crime for what it is, but the horror is that of others; it is only the fear of that horror that is his own.

We are now in a position to understand the nature of the crucial dialogue with his wife that follows: how it is that she gains so speedy a victory over him. She receives his 'golden opinions' speech with savage contempt, accusing him of cowardice. His retort to this, if fear were not his real motive of recoil, would be sound enough, but she quickly exposes it:

MACBETH: Prithee, peace:
I dare do all that may become a man;
Who dares do more is none.

LADY MACBETH: What beast was't then
That made you break this enterprise to me?
When you durst do it, then you were a man;
And, to be more than what you were, you would
Be so much more the man.

It is, in fact, the beast in him that dares, and the man that fears. Knowing as she does the object of the fear is not God or his conscience but public opinion – 'I have bought golden opinions' – it is easy for her to defeat his conscience once and for all. She defeats it, but she does not expel it; it remains within him as the witness, the accuser, of the bestial self that reigns in its room, and by causing his breakdown in the banquet scene of Act III, it ruins them both. Just now, as it is his fear that she has overthrown, so it is her courage that he acclaims:

> Bring forth men-children only;
> For thy undaunted mettle should compose
> Nothing but males.

3. THE MURDERESS

What is the nature of Lady Macbeth's 'courage'? Even less than her husband is she naturally murderous; he, after all, is a soldier for whom bloodshed is inseparable from his profession. She is a woman, a wife, a mother –

> I have given suck, and know
> How tender 'tis to love the babe that milks me

and yet it is she that fears the gentleness of her husband's nature, almost as though it were he that is the woman:

> yet do I fear thy nature;
> It is too full of the milk of human kindness
> To catch the nearest way. . . .

Woman as she is, she finds that it is her task to aid that beast in Macbeth that exists with the womanliness in him – the gentleness in spirit which civilised men have in common with women. This she achieves after a violent repression of the woman in herself:

> Come, you spirits
> That tend on mortal thoughts, unsex me here;
>
> .   .   .   .
>
> Come to my woman's breasts
> And take my milk for gall, you murd'ring ministers. . . .

Milk, thus, is set over against blood – life-giving gentleness over

against murderous ferocity. Blood, however, is ambivalent: a
death symbol outside the body, it is life itself within it; the
movement of the blood (in flushing, for example) reflects
quickness, responsiveness, of feeling. So Lady Macbeth calls on
the spirits to

> make thick my blood,
> Stop up th'access and passage to remorse,
> That no compunctious visitings of nature
> Shake my fell purpose. . . .

The climax of the speech shows that the operation she is under-
taking on her soul is a double one: the woman on the one hand,
heaven on the other, both have to be blind, though indeed to
blind either is to blind each:

> Come, thick night
> And pall thee in the dunnest smoke of hell,
> That my keen knife see not the wound it makes,
> Nor heaven peep through the blanket of the dark,
> To cry 'Hold, hold!'

In this she is close to her husband, who in the previous scene has
ejaculated:

> Stars, hide your fires;
> Let not light see my black and deep desires:
> The eye wink at the hand; yet let that be,
> Which the eye fears, when it is done, to see.

Both hereby admit that the act is incompatible with their
normal, daylight natures, living under the eye of heaven. Yet
there is a difference of rhythm in their speeches, and rhythm
here again is one of the resources of meaning. The rhythm of
Lady Macbeth's speech is impetuous; that of Macbeth's slow
and reflective. Lady Macbeth is seeking to bring about a
radical change in her nature by her words even as she speaks
them, and after their utterance she barely falters until Duncan
is killed. Macbeth, on the other hand, is not seeking to transform himself, for the transformation is coming about from within, involuntarily; the question is whether he will aid it or prevent
it. Here he is aiding it, but the slow, somnambulistic rhythm

67

shows the experience to be traumatic – a sullen submission to what seems inevitable.

Lady Macbeth, then, *seeks* possession by evil; Macbeth *is* possessed. In her, the natural self is thrust down, not denatured. She intends the murder to be a 'perfect' one, with no after-effects beyond those she desires, and, convinced of its feasibility, she can summon up enough resolution to see it through. When, contrary to her expectations, disaster follows disaster as murder succeeds to murder, her resolution slowly fails, and as her true nature returns, it is only that she may sink farther and farther into terror and despair, until she becomes the demented sleep-walker of Act V, and ends 'as tis thought' by taking her own life.

4. SHAKESPEARIAN CHARACTER

Macbeth, perhaps more than any other of Shakespeare's plays, shows the dramatist availing himself of his time's transitional richness of outlook: in its pages the Middle Ages encounter modernity. Spiritually, the tragedy is planned on the medieval scale; it uses the medieval combination of mystery and precision in its moral frame of reference, and it presents its characters with the vastness of implication and assurance of treatment which that frame uniquely affords. A common spiritual light transfuses human nature: Man is, still, more important than men. In the first place a character is Everyman whatever his role; in the second place, he is performing that role, well or ill according to laws that are understood. When he plays it ill, this is because in some way he sets himself against the universal order – not as an individual with idiosyncrasies, but as an individual with the universally shared passions – those appetites which, carried beyond set proportion, make a man the antagonist of God and therefore of other men, and which operate as the role dictates. A king has necessarily the largest role of all to play, and so a good king may approach the status of an ideal man. True, roles in this fallen world sometimes distort men even when they are carried out ideally. One sees in Shakespeare's Henry V how a king may be ideal for his time and society, yet something less than an ideal man. More often, the role offered opportunities for the misuse of man's nature, and so kings are sometimes tyrants, just as lovers like Othello are sometimes murderously jealous. A king who is also a lover, like Leontes in *A Winter's Tale*, may be both.

In *Macbeth*, we have an ideal king in Duncan, and an ideal fighting man in Macbeth. But the soldier's role implies an aggressiveness that may be used destructively, and not merely in the service of his country. Moreover, Macbeth is a nobleman with a consequent highly developed sense of honour, and this may easily become, instead of a guide to conduct, an incitement to extravagant ambition. The true and the false attitudes to honour are concisely shown in the interchange between Macbeth and Banquo, where Macbeth is hinting at a possible collaboration between them:

> MACBETH: If you shall cleave to my consent, – when 'tis,
> It shall make honour for you.
> BANQUO: So I lose none
> In seeking to augment it, but still keep
> My bosom franchis'd, and allegiance clear,
> I shall be counsell'd. (II.i)

Macbeth sees honour as that which is evident, external, just as he attaches all his values to greatness in this world and not at all to spiritual greatness, intelligible only in relation to the next world, where all roles are eliminated in the presence of God. Banquo in his reply shows that he attaches to honour that spiritual significance which allies it to conscience. Honour guided princes and nobles in their duties on earth, but for that very reason it might be falsely identified with mere earthly greatness. Thus we see how Macbeth the nobleman misconstrues his role.

He misconstrues it, as a soldier and as a noble, because his appetites belittle it for the sake of their own acquisitiveness; he is too much the soldier, too much the nobleman, and too little human. In the same way, Lady Macbeth is too much the devoted wife, and represses in herself the woman. Both carry their roles to extremes, and abandon the human nature which keeps them bound to man and God.

The Middle Ages were disposed to ask the question 'What?' –

What is a nobleman? What is a soldier? What is a King?' We on
the other hand are much more inclined to ask 'How?' How does
a good man become a bad one, or a sane woman drive herself
to madness? And it is when we ask the modern question about
Macbeth and Lady Macbeth that we become aware of a new
kind of inwardness, psychological rather than moral, a sequence
of cause and effect that medieval writers did not trace. This new
strain involves awareness of how the dark side of man's nature
operates, and of how ignorance of his nature may lead him to
destruction. Macbeth, as I have tried to show, exemplifies the
first process, and Lady Macbeth the second. The means is
Shakespearian metaphor, verbal symbol, and rhythm, and as
means for such elucidation, they have never been surpassed.

Chapter 4

Lovers by Shakespeare

ANTONY AND CLEOPATRA

1. SHAKESPEARE'S TRAGEDIES OF LOVE

T HE third and last of the great tragedies of love differs from the others in two outstanding ways. First, whereas *Romeo and Juliet* leaves Juliet's impress on the mind, and *Othello* leaves Othello's, one cannot think of *Antony and Cleopatra* without recalling both lovers equally. Secondly, in the earlier plays the lovers' predicaments arise from isolation: Romeo and Juliet try to shed their families and to meet in a new dimension where only their love is real; Desdemona, the dutiful daughter, abandons her father in a way so improbable that he can only account for it by witchcraft, in order to marry a mercenary and outsider, well aware himself that he doesn't 'belong'. In *Antony and Cleopatra*, on the other hand, it is the involvement of each lover in a larger world that precisely matters: Cleopatra, as Queen of Egypt, embodies a way of life, and Antony is one of the two supreme Romances. Both isolation and involvement indeed affect all three plays, in the sense that on the one hand Romeo and Juliet cannot ignore their families and Othello is a Venetian admiral though without any part in Venetian society, while, on the other, the love of Antony and Cleopatra is constantly trying to free itself of the responsibilities of the General and the diplomacy of the Queen. The difference is that these lovers do not really want this liberation to succeed. Antony may declaim

> Let Rome in Tiber melt, and the wide arch
> Of the rang'd Empire fall! Here is my space . . .

or Cleopatra may stammer, when he returns to politics –

> Courteous lord, one word:
> Sir, you and I must part, but that's not it:
> Sir, you and I have lov'd, but there's not it;
> That you know well, something it is I would, –

71

O my oblivion is a very Antony,
And I am all forgotten.

– none the less it is still the fabulous in each other that they adore, and what is fabulous in each is the civilisation which each embodies, and even transcends, but cannot escape.

2. THE TRANSCENDENT CHARACTER: ANTONY

The play is an example of Shakespeare finding a basis for his characterisation in historical portraiture. He used North's translation of Plutarch's lives, and followed it closely. Much can sometimes be learnt by comparing one of North's scenes with Shakespeare's treatment of it. Here is North's description of Antony's death:

Antonius made her cease her lamenting, and called for wine, either bicause he was athirst, or else for that he thought thereby to hasten his death. When he had dronke, he earnestly prayed her, and perswaded her, that she would seek to save her life, if she could possible, without reproache and dishonour: and that chiefly she should trust Proculeius above any man else about Caesar. And as for him selfe, that she should not lament nor sorrowe for the miserable chaunge of his fortune at the end of his dayes: but rather that she should thinke him the more fortunate, for the former triumphs and honors he had received, considering that while he lived he was the noblest and greatest Prince of the world, and that now he was over come, not cowardly, but valiantly, a Romane by an other Romane. As Antonius gave the last gaspe, Proculeius came that was sent from Caesar.

Here is Shakespeare:

ANTONY: I am dying, Egypt, dying.
Give me some wine and let me speak a little.
CLEOPATRA: No, let me speak, and let me rail so high,
That the false huswife Fortune break her wheel,
Provok'd by my offence.
ANTONY: One word, sweet queen:
Of Caesar seek your honour, with your
safety. O!
CLEOPATRA: They do not go together.

ANTONY: Gentle, hear me,
None about Caesar trust but Proculeius.

CLEOPATRA: My resolution and my hands, I'll trust,
None about Caesar.

ANTONY: The miserable change now at my end
Lament nor sorrow at: but please your
    thoughts
In feeding them with those my former fortunes
Wherein I liv'd: the greatest prince o' the
    world,
The noblest; and do now not basely die,
Not cowardly put off my helmet to
My countryman: a Roman, by a Roman
Valiantly vanquish'd. Now my spirit is going,
I can no more.

CLEOPATRA: Noblest of men, woo't die?
Hast thou no care of me, shall I abide
In this dull world, which in thy absence is
No better than a sty? O, see, my women:
The crown o' the earth doth melt.
                    My Lord?
O wither'd is the garland of the war,
The soldier's pole is fall'n: young boys and girls
Are level now with men: the odds is gone,
And there is nothing left remarkable
Beneath the visiting moon.

Plutarch provides the facts, dispassionately. Just before the quoted passage, Cleopatra has been described as in a frenzy of grief, quite uncontrolled. Antony calls for wine, which is bad for his condition, but he sees an urgent final task for himself, and at best only so much time and energy to undertake it in. He has to bring the Queen to her senses, make her face the facts of her condition, and ensure, if possible, that she continues in command of herself when he is gone. At best he has not long to live, and the more protracted his deathbed, the more unlikely it is that she will retain enough control to manage her extremely hazardous condition. The wine gives him strength to impart some final practical advice, and to leave her with an image of himself which will inspirit rather than distract her.

Shakespeare sticks to these facts; he gives us the same information, except that he makes Proculeius enter some time later. But the facts are mere shells, dry and lifeless; Shakespeare gives them inwardness, and this inwardness is a whole relationship epitomised, a scale that ranges in a few lines from pettiness to grandeur, from hysteria to tragedy.

The dialogue opens with discord. The lovely cadence of 'I am dying, Egypt, dying' is an elegy in itself, and the direct simplicity of the next line makes it the more moving, but Cleopatra responds with the shrill, egotistic execration of 'the huswife Fortune', which Samuel Johnson called despicable and of which another critic says that Cleopatra 'strikes a false note'. She *is* being despicable, but Shakespeare knows what he is doing. Antony has begun by addressing her by the stately title 'Egypt', with its odd mixture of formality and familiarity as of one sovereign speaking to another: he has not forgotten his dignity in this extremity. When she comes back at him in the mode of vulgar melodrama, showing that she is out of touch with both his and her own predicaments, he manœuvres to get closer to her, with the half-tender, but still half-formal 'sweet queen'. However, she keeps to her theatrical, unreal and unrealistic style, and he resorts to the intimate, gracious, tenderly protesting word 'Gentle'. Still, while he is speaking of her, she retains her stagey role in accordance with the image of herself that she has been pleased to adopt, and so at last he builds up the image of himself by which she is to remember him, and by which he wishes to be remembered. Partly, the speech is for his own benefit: he is trying to leave with this world as much as he can of what he values in himself; yet, with it, he finally breaks through to her, and she merges her self-regarding grief in her grief for him. The falseness of her earlier tone lies in her attempt to bolster herself up by self-pity and a posture of defiance which it is not in her nature to sustain. The falseness is the more marked in that it is not the hypothetical goddess Fortune but her own self that has brought Antony low, as she is fully aware; she is fighting against recognition of the real tragedy, which Antony, in lines that are themselves in part self-regarding, brings her, with his last breaths, to acknowledge, though his aim has been to enable her to endure it. Thus there is irony in the pathos: while he speaks only of her, she remains self-regarding; when he becomes self-regarding, her sorrow all flows towards him.

He has had to fight through the self-centred arrogant Queen to the woman, and when the woman responds, it is at first with the tenderness such as any bereaved wife might use: 'Noblest of men, woo't die?' But the lines open out in a grand diapason in which Antony the hero, the embodiment of human greatness, leaves the earth and abandons it to sterility, as though it were forsaken by the sun itself and knew only the bleak light of the moon: while the sun rears and nourishes, the moon only 'visits', prying with her cold useless light. This is true grandeur, after the false grandeur of the Queen railing at fortune, and after the grandeur modified by the pathetic self-regard of Antony's final speech. It is also truly and greatly human: the woman at last brought to terms with the Queen, as well as with the kingly lover.

Cleopatra ruined Antony, the warrior-prince, by rendering him helpless in everything except his love for her, but she knows quite well what it is that she has ruined. It is the tragic paradox that Antony's greatness, humanly understood, would have been diminished had he not sacrificed all to his mistress, and had his mistress not understood the extent of the sacrifice.

It is as though Shakespeare were answering the question: 'What sort of greatness does a human being achieve, when he lives out to the full all his passionate impulses?' Before judging the answer, we have to limit its terms in two ways. The first is that, while we are obviously not here concerned with a saint, some standard of sanctity seems none the less needful in order that 'greatness' and 'human' may have meaning. If we compare Antony on the one hand to a character who is merely more successful, such as his rival Octavius Caesar, we find that we have to subtract from Antony in order to arrive at an image on Octavius' level; Octavius, and also his sister Octavia of the 'still, holy, and cold conversation', are less than fully human. If, on the other hand, Antony is thought of as merely indulging his impulses – mutually destructive, moreover, as they are – then it is hard to see him as great. We have to find a common factor behind Antony's impulses, and one not liable to destruction. This factor is Antony's generosity, his capacity to *give* himself, and not merely to yield himself, to everything he does, every role he adopts. Now this capacity to give oneself implies sainthood; but his times are pagan, and the alternative to being merely human is not present for Antony, who is thus irrevocably the hero-lover.

This basic quality of generosity in living is also to be found in Plutarch's account of Antony. One of Shakespeare's achievements is to present the quality in such a way as to fuse it with the Renaissance image of the Great Man – the man who triumphs in war and love, and whose dignity remains undiminished in loss and death. This is the second limitation we must make in judging Shakespeare's answer to the question: he answers it in Renaissance terms.

In every age, the ultimate in human greatness, regarded as sheer fulfilment of energies, demands for its proper expression some conception of an adequate pole of attraction. The Renaissance was an age when the surrender of the human to the divine had to compete, in its hold on the human imagination, with the appeal of the surrender to earthly splendour. Competing against both, with all the force of medieval romance behind it, was the dream of the flesh, of the ideal mistress who made all else stale. The realisation of such a dream is Shakespeare's Cleopatra.

3. THE TRANSCENDENT CHARACTER: CLEOPATRA

Antony, at the opening of the play, is fully in her power, oblivious to political drama, forgetful of military tasks. Not surprisingly, his outraged officers refer to the Queen with vigorous contempt. She has a 'tawny front'; Antony has become 'the bellows and the fan to cool a gipsy's lust', and 'a strumpet's fool'. Suchlike is the view of her natural enemies; how is she seen by her admirers? North's Plutarch is again worth quoting: 'Now her beawtie . . . was not so passing, as unmatchable of other women, nor yet suche, as upon present view did enamor men with her: but so sweet was her companie and conversacion, that a man could not possibly but be taken.' Accordingly, there is little if any mention of her beauty in the play, but constant examples of her wit. However, wit is seldom enough to amount to a fatal attraction. Her distinctive quality, which Shakespeare adapts and expands from Plutarch, is her variety. Antony, in the first scene, says to her:

> Fie, wrangling queen!
> Whom everything becomes, to chide, to laugh,
> To weep: how every passion fully strives
> To make itself, in thee, fair and admired!

This is her lover speaking, but Enobarbus, his most devoted follower, and as concerned as any about the menace she constitutes to his General's fortunes, says of her in II, ii:

> Age cannot wither her, nor custom stale
> Her infinite variety: other women cloy
> The appetites they feed, but she makes hungry,
> Where most she satisfies. For vilest things
> Become themselves in her, that the holy priests
> Bless her, when she is riggish. (I.e. wanton.)

To this Maecenas replies:

> If beauty, wisdom, modesty, can settle
> The heart of Antony, Octavia is
> A blessed lottery to him.

Octavia is a paragon of physical and moral beauty, whereas Cleopatra is not strikingly beautiful, and harbours 'vile' qualities. But whereas Octavia has been given to Antony in diplomatic marriage – the fortunes of politics have brought them together – Cleopatra is in the nature of Fate herself. Antony remarks 'how every passion fully strives to make itself, in thee, fair and admired', as though she were a kind of heaven for the passions, where they were still themselves and yet redeemed; and Enobarbus, that 'vilest things become themselves in her', i.e. appear attractive though without altering their nature. Cleopatra is in her own nature not only a world but a paradise, and a realm where the ordinary critical faculties cease to operate.

So far we have looked at her reflections, in the distorting mirrors of her enemies, the flattering mirrors of her admirers. How does she appear to us, the audience, in direct impression? How does Shakespeare convey dramatically this woman whose 'infinite variety' . . . 'makes hungry Where most she satisfies'?

Before we attempt an assessment of her, we must observe a precaution which, though it may seem too obvious to need mentioning, is very often neglected by modern readers. For reasons partly connected with the nineteenth-century development of realism in stage production, partly with reading habits more appropriate to the novel, and most of all with critical attitudes inherited from the romantics, we are very inclined to assume, first, that major fictitious characters are whole beings, assessable separately from their contexts, and, second, that such characters must (when they are not 'bad') so magnetise our sympathies that we end by identifying ourselves with them. In this way we lose the capacity to feel a drama as an event outside our sympathies, yet involving our emotions. We do not allow a character his or her own nature, because we are taking for granted that he or she is to behave in accordance with our own ideal behaviour in the same situation. When the character's behaviour becomes incongruous from this viewpoint, we in turn become confused or censorious; or we theorise about the action in such a way as to make away with our difficulties rather than to enlarge our understanding. But Shakespeare's characterisation is on different principles. In the first place, his stage was susceptible to methods of illusion but not to those of delusion: his audiences could watch his plays as a crowd might witness a mirage in a desert, aware that they were not seeing real water, but not as a cinema audience watches a film in a darkened auditorium, almost oblivious to their lives outside it. And secondly, the body of assumptions on which his plays were based were metaphysical rather than psychological; at all events, his psychology was not intelligible without his metaphysics.

When we return to Cleopatra, with these reservations to our power to estimate her in our minds, we find that we can only determine what she is in the light of what she is to Antony and

Antony to her; this again requires us to consider what Antony was to Rome, and Rome to Shakespeare as he shows it to us in the play. Her part only makes sense as an element of that whole. And secondly, when we have related the part to the whole, we shall find that it is too large in its scope for us to identify ourselves with it; we should have to be both more and less than human, for Cleopatra embodies a mode of existence purified from the alloys which in an actual being modify it. She is the life of the senses in its female manifestation, set in a context of masculine rivalries, from participation in which her nature excludes her, and yet, because they are masculine, in which she is inexorably involved.

We are left with the question of what impact she makes on us in detail. We find that she is protean, beginning a scene in one mood, ending it in another, and exhibiting a third in passing. Yet she is consistent, and her consistency is of three kinds: whatever faults or virtues she exhibits, they are always those of a woman; she is instantly responsive to impulse; and she is ever guileful. The last two qualities would seem to be incompatible; but in her the guile runs so deep – Antony calls her his 'serpent of old Nile', and speaks of her as 'cunning past man's thought' – that it does not inhibit the impulse, but only calls in question, not so much whether she is ever speaking sincerely, as whether sincerity in Cleopatra, like everything else, does not have a peculiar significance. Thus in I, iii, when Antony is leaving her for the first time and she chooses to suppose that he is doing it at the behest of his wife Fulvia – in fact, dead, as she learns halfway through the scene – she begins by addressing him with mocking raillery, so light, and yet so cutting, that he does not know how to take it, and neither do we. Then a flash breaks from her of genuine anger –

> I would I had thy inches; thou shouldst know
> There were a heart in Egypt.

– which causes him to break in firmly with the news of his wife's death. This, instead of disconcerting her, causes her to return to a new vein of mockery, which suddenly collapses into the stammering, heartfelt speech beginning 'Courteous lord . . .'

79

that I have already quoted. She seems now the simple, heart-broken woman, stricken at being forsaken by her lover. Bewildered, he replies with –

> But that your royalty
> Holds idleness your subject, I should take you
> For idleness itself.

Thereupon she seems to recover, and ends with a farewell of pathos, which is yet calm and dignified, and in which irony only adds to sadness:

> 'Tis sweating labour
> To bear such idleness so near the heart
> As Cleopatra this. But, sir, forgive me;
> Since my becomings kill me, when they do not
> Eye well to you: your honour calls you hence;
> Therefore be deaf to my unpitied folly,
> And all the gods go with you! upon your sword
> Sit laurel victory! and smooth success
> Be strewed before your feet!

Does she, then, reach sincerity in these last two speeches, or are they part of her unending tactics to keep Antony enslaved, to make sure that even though he leaves her he must return? It is characteristic of her that it should be both; she is speaking with deep feeling, yet calculating her words, just as her earlier mockery was nicely measured, yet expressive of deep anger. Guile in Cleopatra is not acquired, but instinctive.

Totally feminine as she is, she is without physical courage, yet guile too is an element of her cowardice. When her fleet joins Antony's against the Romans in the battle of Actium, she suddenly turns her galley about before battle is engaged, and her action causes a general demoralisation and rout. She protests that she never thought her action would affect Antony himself, but he replies:

> Egypt, thou knewst too well
> My heart was to thy rudder tied by the strings,
> And thou shouldst tow me after: o'er my spirit
> Thy full supremacy thou knew'st, and that
> Thy beck might from the bidding of the gods
> Command me.

The fact is that she could not allow him to win the battle, for if he did, Rome would have claimed him again, there would have been another treaty, and Antony would have been induced to return to Octavia. It is not to be thought that Cleopatra consciously engineers Antony's defeat, but what she 'knows too well' she does not necessarily make explicit to herself.

The single word 'cowardice', or a kinder synonym, is also insufficient to explain her postponement of death. It distinguishes her from Antony, who dies of a wound inflicted on himself in consequence of the false report of Cleopatra's death put about by herself, as it does from Shakespeare's other tragic lovers. Othello kills himself immediately on discovering his mistake about Desdemona; Romeo and Juliet die together; but though, at the end of Act IV, Cleopatra declares her intention to follow Antony, we find in Act V, i, as in Plutarch, that she has sent a messenger to inquire into Caesar's intentions. The delay was imposed on Shakespeare both by the chronicle and by art: by the chronicle, because the facts of the story were too well known through it for Shakespeare to ignore them in so important a particular, and by art, because the opposition of her nature to Antony's demands for her a different kind of death, and one which could not be huddled on top of his. Accordingly, Cleopatra is only reconciled to death when she becomes certain that Caesar intends to use her as an exhibit in the triumphal pageant which is to celebrate his return to Rome.

> Nay, 'tis most certain, Iras: – saucy lictors
> Will catch at us, like strumpets; and scald rimers
> Ballad us out o' tune: the quick comedians
> Extemporally will stage us, and present
> Our Alexandrian revels; Antony
> Shall be brought drunken forth, and I shall see
> Some squeaking Cleopatra boy my greatness
> I' the posture of a whore.

Their love has been an absolute, its own Heaven, which death cannot contradict, though such ignominy could:

> Show me, my women, like a queen: – go fetch
> My best attires; – I am again for Cydnus,
> To meet Mark Antony. . . .

Her fluent, ever-changeful nature now coheres into form as
clear and firm as Octavia's –

> My resolution's plac'd, and I have nothing
> Of woman in me: now from head to foot
> I am marble-constant; now the fleeting moon
> No planet is of mine.

She had imaged the exhilaration of all the senses; she had
embodied that immediacy of experience which captivated the
Renaissance as it had captivated Antony. Her death is in keeping, for it too is a sensual fulfilment:

> As sweet as balm, as soft as air, as gentle –
> O Antony! . . .

4. ROME AND EGYPT: THE TWO CLIMATES

J. F. Danby has described Rome and Egypt as standing in the
tragedy for the World and the Flesh. It is obvious that they
stand for far more than do the Montagues and Capulets in
Romeo and Juliet, or even Venice in *Othello*. But Rome is in one
sense greater than Antony, and in another sense lesser; Egypt,
on the other hand, is subsumed in Cleopatra.

As only one of the rulers of the Empire, Antony has to fight,
compete, and conspire against the others, especially Octavius.
The stake, as the antagonists see it, is world rule; the qualities
admired are aptitude for intrigue, shown notably by Octavius
Caesar, and the virtues of the soldier, – the disinterestedness in
service of Ventidius, the devotion of Enobarbus, the strength,
courage and endurance of Antony. This is a highly disciplined,
cold world, in which affection is subjected to duty and duty to
ambition: Octavius loves his sister, but uses her as a pawn in
party politics. Octavia herself, the representative woman of the
system, is tailored to the Roman conception of virtue as seen
by her menfolk. It is an admirable world, for the virtues it
nourishes are lofty and revered for their own sake; yet it is far
from wholly admirable, for the same virtues are always in
danger of sacrifice or perversion for the sake of ambition.
Ventidius has to halt his campaigns for fear of arousing Antony's
jealousy, and Enobarbus, of all people, eventually betrays his

master in order to save his own career. The air of Rome is thin, and not as pure as it is supposed to be.

The world of Egypt – of Alexandria and Cleopatra's court – has none of these virtues. Iris and Charmian are utterly faithful to Cleopatra, but their devotion is different from that of Roman officers to their General: they die with her because they would have no existence without her, whereas Enobarbus kills himself sheerly from shame at his desertion. Instead, it has an intense life of the senses, such as the Roman world knows nothing of. The nucleus of this life is Cleopatra herself, and its essence is concentrated in Enobarbus' famous description of her in her barge (II, ii). Critics have observed that this description might well be cloying in its intensive assault on the senses by sight, sound, scent and tactility, but that it is on the contrary permeated with liveliness. Cleopatra's enchantment intoxicates the moral faculties into inertia, but it alerts the physical ones; it is Antony, left alone 'enthroned i' the market-place . . . Whistling to the air', who is inert. Rome has 'gravitas', but Egypt has buoyancy:

> A strange invisible perfume hits the sense. . . .

Coleridge said that opposites are complementary, but that contraries are mutually destructive. Rome and Egypt are contraries: each demands sole empire. Cleopatra is to Octavius an ornament for his triumph, his most expensive piece of booty; Cleopatra can only hold Antony by ruining him as a Roman. It is his Roman side of him that turns away from her –

> He was dispos'd to mirth; but on the sudden
> A Roman thought hath struck him. (I, ii.)

and may even turn against her in violent revulsion –

> I found you as a morsel, cold upon
> Dead Caesar's trencher: nay you were a fragment
> Of Gnaeus Pompey's, besides what hotter hours,
> Unregister'd in vulgar fame, you have
> Luxuriously picked out. For I am sure,
> Though you can guess what temperance should be,
> You know not what it is.

Plutarch observes how Antony proved the saying 'that the soule of a lover lived in another body, and not in his owne'. He gives himself to Cleopatra, and his soul is indeed hers, but it is at the same time a Roman soul, sometimes resentful, sometimes languishing, and either most when he faces his own failure as a Roman. In the following lines, after Actium, the conflict in him is apparent:

CLEOPATRA: Pardon, pardon!
ANTONY: Fall not a tear, I say, one of them rates
        All that is won and lost: give me a kiss,
        Even this repays me. We sent our school-
        master,
        Is a' come back? Love, I am full of lead:
        Some wine within there, and our viands!
        Fortune knows
        We scorn her most, when most she offers blows.

Cleopatra's kiss 'repays' him, but it is a coin which has no exchange in Roman currency. To revive his spirits he calls for wine, and it is not the only time. His Roman soul pines in her as in a tomb, as it is on her actual tomb that he dies.

Yet Cleopatra arouses no mere rage of the senses; she is associated with fertility, just as she is associated with the fertilising Nile. After Enobarbus' description of her in her barge, the Roman Agrippa remarks of her, brutally but splendidly:

    Royal wench!
She made great Caesar lay his sword to bed;
He plough'd her, and she cropp'd.

That is, she had a son by the great Julius. The line assimilates her to mother earth. But we see her only once behaving as a mother, and then the 'child' is the death-bringing asp.

Rome and Egypt are the worlds of the male and the female, each asserting dominance on its own terms, and intriguing to secure it. Octavius and Cleopatra have in common only that both are tireless intriguers; when they meet at the end of the play, it is to intrigue against each other, and it is Octavius who is outwitted. Antony is the most masculine of all Shakespeare's heroes except Coriolanus; he has Alcides – Hercules – the most

masculine hero of myth, as his legendary ancestor. In this
tragedy he is the victim of the war between the masculine and
feminine cultures; he is deprived of his leadership of the
masculine world by the leader of the feminine world. Antony
and Cleopatra figure the opposite sides in the deepest cleavage
in human nature, – when, that is, the difference is of contraries
and not of opposites – the ultimate male and female. We are still
not far from character seen as every man and every woman.

Part 2

The Emergence of Loneliness

Chapter 5

Milton's Satan

I. SATAN AND PARADISE LOST

EVERYONE knows that, however difficult it may be to enjoy *Paradise Lost* throughout, the first two books are splendid because of the grandeur of Satan. Only he among all the figures in the cast fully imposes himself on our imaginations, and even he only in these books. Everyone who knows anything of the poem knows too of the great debates that have revolved round the paradox that, impressive as he is, this impressiveness is not exactly one of incarnate evil. We know that he is evil, because he is Satan, and because Milton is concerned to 'justifie the wayes of God to men'. We may even feel that he is evil, but we feel other things about him too; in particular, he extorts our admiration, and even our sympathy.

What did Milton intend by giving the Devil so rich an emotional substance, and no one else? Did he understand what he was doing, or was he unconsciously bedevilled? To follow such questions is to involve oneself in the doctrinal problems of the whole poem, and that is here impracticable. A question we must follow, however, is whether a character of Satan's complexity has any rightful place in such a poem at all.

Character, after all, implies definition. A character may have immense variety like Cleopatra, or may be vastly representative, like Criseyde, but like a country with distinctive geography, climate, and customs it imposes its limits upon us; we know when we are there, when we are not. But if a narrative figure is by its nature unknowable, or if its representativeness is so vast as to comprehend phenomena too various to be known, then definition of this kind is impossible. On the one hand, neither God nor the Angels can have character; on the other, Adam and Eve, as the parent of all mankind, are the germ of all mankind, and therefore indefinable. Satan would then seem to be

89

doubly indefinable: he is an angel, and so by his nature unknowable, and he is the source of all evil, and evil, once we
admit its positive existence, is as mysterious, various, and almost
as illimitable, as the goodness of God. Thus Satan, by being
made a character, is made to concrete a force which we feel to
be in its nature diffused, to be intolerant of limits. He is, however, doctrinally defined through his fall, since this came about
through his commission of the original sin – he fell through
Pride.

2. THE CHARACTER OF SATAN

The reader of the first two books of *Paradise Lost*, then, has to
endure a double vision. There is the theological vision: God's
flawless creation is fractured by Satan's pride. His pride led to
rebellion, and his rebellion brought death and sin into the
universe. At the beginning of the poem, as he lies transfixed in
the fiery lake, he is by no means a tragic figure but the evidence
that we need not, in spite of him and appearances, despair; for
though the war is long the decisive victory of Good over Evil
was accomplished before ever humanity became participant in
the struggle. We know that Milton must intend this, and if we
didn't know, we would infer it from the invocation to Book I.

But after the invocation, this Vision becomes overlaid by
quite another. Satan turns his head and addresses Beelzebub
who lies beside him:

> If thou beest he; But O how fall'n! how chang'd
> From him, who in the happy Realms of Light
> Cloth'd with transcendent brightness didst outshine
> Myriads though bright: If he whom mutual league,
> United thoughts and counsels, equal hope,
> And hazard in the Glorious Enterprize,
> Joynd with me once, now misery hath joynd
> In equal ruin: into what Pit thou seest
> From what highth fall'n, so much the stronger provd
> He with his Thunder: and till then who knew
> The force of those dire Arms?

The epic vision has screened the doctrinal one. 'He with his

Thunder' might better be Zeus, removed from humanity by power rather than wisdom and love. 'He with his Thunder' has overthrown the brightest of the Angels, united in the brotherhood of 'the Glorious Enterprize', united now in the brotherhood of common defeat. Milton clearly does not intend that we should forget the doctrinal Truth of truths which belies Satan's words, but while we may still hold that with our intellect, our imagination is beginning to tell us a different story. Satan, as he goes on, gathers strength; though defeated, he is not abject:

> yet not for those
> Nor what the Potent Victor in his rage
> Can else inflict do I repent or change,
> Though chang'd in outward lustre; that fixt mind
> And high disdain, from sense of injur'd merit,
> That with the mightiest rais'd me to contend,
> And to the fierce contention brought along
> Innumerable force of Spirits arm'd
> That durst dislike his reign, and me preferring,
> His utmost power with adverse power oppos'd
> In dubious Battel on the Plains of Heav'n
> And shook his throne.

Doctrine and reason alike tell us that Satan is implausible. We know that this is not a case of injured merit, and that God's throne is unshakable. But he is not tempting us, unless through Milton's mind; he is inspiriting his brother in defeat. That is to say, he is, to our imaginations, less a spirit than a hero, able to meet that supreme test of heroism – refusal to despair even in desperation. Doctrine will retort that on the contrary Satan *is* despairing – that the ultimate form of despair is obduracy to God. But by this time, the lines of epic and doctrine are hopelessly crossed: doctrine refutes epic, but epic holds our attention. In the lines just quoted, admittedly, it does so more by overlaying our usual conceptions of the devil than by eloquence – the idea of Satan of all creatures maintaining 'injured merit' is so incongruous, even if it be one of his most subtle temptations to induce man to do so. But in the lines that follow, we have the classic declaration of the great resistance leader:

What though the field be lost?
All is not lost; the unconquerable Will,
And study of revenge, immortal hate,
And courage never to submit or yield:
And what is else not to be overcome?
That Glory never shall his wrath or might
Extort from me.

With these lines, doctrine is routed. We know that Satan has been overwhelmed. His penalty is far more terrible than any a human rebel could receive, for he faces not only eternity of torment, but eternal loss of supreme bliss. But this has happened because he has rebelled against a despotic universe: God is a Tyrant who exacted utter submission, and Satan has challenged the premise on which the justice of that exaction is based. Moreover, he still challenges it, and offsets degradation, torment and loss with pride of defiance and glory of self-possession. This is not the Devil who is the Author of all meanness and suffering; this is the Father of heroes who lose all but retain the empires of their own souls.

This impression is not lessened when he replies to the despondent Beelzebub with an oath that 'ever to do ill' will be 'our sole delight'. The 'ill' that he will do remains at present hypothetical; what we feel about Satan is that he is dynamic; that God may be against him, but that he is life-enhancing. The retort that Hitler no doubt affected his audiences similarly, can be met: Hitler used degrading means. Satan may be undermining the doctrine of the poem, but he is not undermining ours, or whatever we have that makes for nobility in our natures.

After a description of Satan's huge dimensions as he lies 'Prone on the Flood', doctrine makes a return by pointing out that Satan is to be 'enrag'd' at finding that all his evil will only serve to demonstrate 'Infinite goodness', but epic retaliates by describing Satan rising from the fiery flood with all the majestic grace of a great bird:

Forthwith he rears from off the Pool
His mighty Stature; on each hand the flames
Driven backward slope their pointing spires, and rowld
In billows, leave i'th'midst a horrid vale.

92

> Then with expanded wings he stears his flight
> Aloft, incumbent on the dusky Air
> That felt unusual weight, till on dry Land
> He lights . . .

He commands the hellish element that is supposed to command him with that effect of triumphant ease that an eagle has over the heavenly one, and again doctrine has spoken vainly in having pointed out that it is Heaven that enables this. The mechanics of Heaven's enablement is beyond the imagination; Satan *doing* it is not.

Alighting, he surveys the landscape of infinite desolation, and accepts it as his realm, renouncing 'the happy Fields where Joy for ever dwells', and declaring with the sort of pride which, because it is inspiring, it is very difficult to think of as sinful:

> The mind is its own place, and in itself
> Can make a Heav'n of Hell, a Hell of Heav'n.

As he summons the many legions of fallen angels about him, and surveys them in his ravaged magnificence, we have, I think, an example of doctrine trying to insert itself into the epic description:

> Dark'n'd so, yet shon
> Above them all th'Arch Angel: but his face
> Deep scars of Thunder had intrencht, and care
> Sat on his faded cheek, but under Browes
> Of dauntless courage, and considerate Pride
> Waiting revenge: cruel his eye, but cast
> Signs of remorse and passion to behold
> The fellows of his crime, the followers rather
> (Far other once beheld in bliss) condemn'd
> For ever now to have their lot in pain,
> Millions of Spirits for his fault amerc't
> Of Heav'n, and from Eternal Splendors flung
> For his revolt, yet faithfull how they stood
> Thir Glory witherd.

'Cruel his eye', yet casting 'Signs of remorse and passion'.... Is not 'cruel' inserted to remind us that this is a horrifying, not an admirable being, that the remorse and passion can have nothing about them commensurate with love? It is as though Milton's doctrine were concerned lest we may respond with inconvenient alacrity to an epic vision of the war-scarred veteran, unsubdued by defeat, and surrounded by followers who still devote to him that unhellish virtue, trust. 'Cruel', at all event, doesn't sit very easily with 'remorse'. There are other touches which seem to show Milton's doctrine to be trying to present Satan as horrific rather than impressive; perhaps the earlier description of him talking to Beelzebub with eyes that 'sparkling blaz'd' – to which T. S. Eliot takes an exception – is an example.

'The great consult' that follows the uprising of the City of Pandemonium is like any other Council of War in a defeated army, and once the future strategy has been decided – to invade the Earth – it is Satan who undertakes the formidable adventure of finding this new creation. Before he can get out of Hell, he has to face the weird figures of Sin and Death. Their monstrosity, and the complicated enormity of their relationship with Satan are too remote from human experience to befoul his image for us, though they enlarge it with mystery. His flight through Chaos sustains his effect of grandeur – though it is perhaps sobering to think of Satan as the first Space Traveller – so that one participates in the achievement as he comes sailing into the upper atmosphere:

> and now with ease
> Wafts on the calmer wave by dubious light
> And like a weather-beaten Vessel holds
> Gladly the Port, though Shrouds and Tackle torn;
> Or in the emptier waste, resembling Air
> Weighs his spread wings, at leasure to behold. . . .

We never see this Satan again. He is henceforth a different being, for the reason that henceforth – except for a brief glimpse in Book X – we meet him out of his element. Once on Earth or (as before his fall) in Heaven, he has to conform to the generalised quality of the other figures in the poem, from God the Father to Eve. But he has made his ineffaceable impression, such that he has thrown the rest of the epic out of perspective.

3. THE UNFURNISHED UNIVERSE

It has been said that Shakespeare lived in a world of time, and Milton in a universe of space. The comparison is to Milton's disadvantage, for Shakespeare's treatment of time is immensely varied and subtle, whereas Miltonic space, whatever its grandeur, is somewhat simplified. None the less, Miltonic space has importance beyond its function as mere setting – an importance which extends to the theme of character.

Dante, in his *Divine Comedy*, also inhabited a universe of space, but the difference between his space and Milton's is significant: Miltonic space is vast and empty; Dantesque space is filled. For Dante, Hell is within the earth, and Purgatory is a mountain which Virgil reaches by penetrating Hell. The circling spheres of the planets and the sun surround the earth, and these are the outer regions of Heaven, filled with blessed spirits and merging into the infinite, God-filled Heaven of Heavens. For Milton, Heaven is very far above the earth as Hell is very far below it, and Chaos separates not only the earth from Hell but Heaven from the circling spheres, which are empty but for a purified atmosphere irradiated with light. However, Earth is suspended from Heaven by a golden chain, and Sin and Death build a causeway up to it over Chaos, in the tracks of Satan.

The invention of the telescope no doubt assisted Milton in his conception of space, and the Reformation accounts for the absence of Purgatory in his cosmography; moreover, there has of course been no time to fill the universe with spirits, blessed and damned. The important differences between the poets cannot, however, be reached by way of such considerations. It is not merely a matter of fullness and emptiness of regions and souls; indeed, so far as mere matter goes, Milton's chaos is hideously crowded. Emptiness, apart from Limbo, has no part in Dante's vision because his universe is filled with meaning; even Limbo is dense with souls unworthy to be damned – that is to say, even meaninglessness has a meaning in Dante's conception. But in Milton's universe, vast regions have no meaning at all, or – as in the spheres surrounding the earth – only a very rarefied meaning as an atmosphere which created beings may inhabit. Dante's Hell is full of concentrated meanings all carefully defined and distinguished, whereas the immense emptiness which Milton's appalled demons explore is the stuff of meaninglessness. This, and not the liquid and solid fire of its consistency, is what captures the imagination as being Hell indeed. Some of Shakespeare's characters reach it: Lear discerns nothingness; Macbeth in his 'Tomorrow and tomorrow' expounds the emptiness of time. But these are meaningful beings in ruin: in *Paradise Lost* we have absence of meaning in itself, as chaos and void.

Meaningfulness, then, in *Paradise Lost* is a quality which is encountered – one crosses a frontier into it as a traveller passes from desert into fertility. It is not, as with Dante, the very substance of the universe. This accounts for the contrasting treatment by the two poets of God and Satan. God is presented directly in the last canto of the Paradiso as a sphere of radiance, yet the image is the imaginative focus for the entire poem; Satan is presented in the last Canto of the Inferno – a vast, static, weeping being, three-headed, with a sinner in each jaw and batwings beating the air. In one aspect he is little more than a cosmographical focal point; in another he is the chief of the damned. Milton's God on the other hand is a strangely finite figure: omnipotent, but autocratic; as anthropomorphic as Jupiter; as finite to perception as any creature. In brief, Dante's God is all-pervasive whereas his Satan is inert; Milton's God is self-withheld so that his Satan can abound.

Milton, of course, is concerned with the how and why of beginnings, whereas Dante is concerned with ends – ends regarded as conclusions less than as purposes, as what human beings do with themselves, and what the consequences are of their choices. Dante begins with an identifiable man – himself – in middle age in the middle of a savage wood. Milton begins with an invocation to launch him on his task, which is to justify the ways of God to Man.

No doubt we must beware of taking Milton's 'justifie' in the polemical sense: he is not aiming at the conversion of unbelievers by rational demonstration. He is seeking by imaginative means to prepare men's hearts to receive God's Provi-

dence. However, he has chosen to do this through the form of
the classical epic, and the classical epic implied such themes as
salvation after peril, achievement through, or in spite of,
destruction, creation in the midst of conflict. So we are shown
the universe as a vast field of war in which we are infinitely
involved, and in which it is therefore crucial that we should
choose the right side. Choosing the wrong side, however, is not
likely to mean consciously choosing Satan's – a course not often
taken. Almost certainly, it will mean to repeat the satanic error
of defining oneself against God.

This was the mistake which Satan seduced Eve into making,
and to which we are hereditarily susceptible. And the effect of
thus cutting ourselves off from the Creator is that we also sever
ourselves from our fellow-creatures, except where self-interests
combine. 'Society' is the name for such a combination of self-
interests, and Milton was writing on the brink of an age in
which men were to talk, act and think in terms of Society more
and more, up to our own time. More and more, Society was to
be in the literal sense Godless: not actively against God, but
dispensing with him. The characteristic art form of Society was
to be the novel, and the novel has been defined as 'the epic of
man without God'.

4. THE MILTONIC HELL AND HUMAN SOCIETY

Satan in Hell – as Milton presents him – is the paradigm for
Man in Society, as he is to be exhibited in the novel.

This view, of course, in no sense conveys Milton's intentions.
Far from opening the way for a new form of art, Milton is using
a very old form for a conservative purpose. It is Adam, not
Satan, who is the central figure in the story, and as L. A.
Cormican[1] says, the story 'is the last of the medieval attempts to
write the history of Everyman, to survey the whole course of
events from the Creation to man's final ascent into Heaven, and
to relate this course to the universal plan of Divine Providence'.
On the other hand, *Paradise Lost* was written – like *Pilgrim's
Progress* – at one of those critical moments in cultural history
when it is possible, through a sort of collision between the

[1] *Pelican Guide to English Literature*, Vol. 3.

imagination and more conscious parts of the mind, for a creative work to be more revolutionary than the writer knows; when such works may exhibit unawares turning points in mental evolution.

We have seen that it is the great emptiness of Hell that makes for its peculiar hellishness, but we must remember that the fallen angels 'civilised' it. They raised up the city of Pandemonium –

> Not Babilon
> Nor great Alcairo such magnificence
> Equal'd in all thir glories.

They already had a form of social organisation, partly the remains of heavenly hierarchies, partly the result of military organisation required by the War in Heaven; partly, by submission to Satan.

> O shame to men! Devil with Devil damn'd
> Firm concord holds, men onely disagree
> Of Creatures rational, though under hope
> Of heavenly Grace. . . :

Finally, in the absence of Satan on his long journey, they organise their activities – athletic, military, artistic, philosophical, exploratory. We forget that Hell is a region of dense blackness and lurid flame, and some at least of the appalling emptiness begins to fill. Hell becomes a parody of Heaven. The whole structure is ultimately vain –

> Vain wisdom all, and false Philosophie

but it is an elaborate and ingenious makeshift for collaborative self-deception.

'An ingenious makeshift for collaborative self-deception' – Society is undeniably more than this, yet this, in the novels of Jane Austen as much as anywhere, is one of its aspects; her characters, for instance in *Sense and Sensibility*, can often be divided between those who come to see through the deception and those who do not. The theme is capable of immensely various treatment, but in some form or other, the tension between the inertia of society, as it seeks to come to rest in its own false sufficiency, and the life-force of the individual as he seeks to achieve his own true sufficiency, is I believe basic to every major novel. And in any version, there seem to be two minimal requirements for success: the author must show his character as under authentic social pressures, and he must have a vision of human potentiality which exceeds social limits.

5. THE APPEAL OF SATAN

The new fall of man in the seventeenth century, when reason began to displace imagination, when scientific modes of knowing began to overlay religious ones, when society began simultaneously to fragment and to constitute a new absolute, when men began to lose the sense of inclusion within a great continuum from rocks to God, when, in short, Everyman turned into Robinson Crusoe – these great changes were at once a great loss and a great release. On the one hand, poets on the scale of Dante and Shakespeare, or, for that matter, of Chaucer, ceased, for to have such poets it is necessary to have a cosmos of language cognate with a cosmos of being, so that the mind can travel to its limits using language as its element, and remain coherent. So characters which figure in themselves extremes of the greatness and littleness of man – characters like Criseyde, Cleopatra, Macbeth – these were both too simple and too profound for the new kind of creativity. Humanity began to be felt in its particularity as never before, and the fact, that each man was seen to have his personal drama, transferred to the individual much of that eloquence of life which was fading from the image of Man as Mankind. More and more, too, Society was seen to be dependent for its authentic life on what is in the individual, and, at the same time it was seen that the individual needs to nourish his vitality from sources which Society can neither constrain nor contain. These are the sources, in 'nature' or in 'God' or both in one, which were accessible to the older societies through their conscious dependence on them, but were becoming increasingly obstructed in the new Society by its assumption of autonomy.

Thus the individual in this new Society has been both at home and not at home; it has been his kingdom and his prison.

Sometimes he has fought against it and sought another realm; sometimes he has fought to remain in it against the forces magnetising him (within and outside himself) from beyond its reach. It has maltreated him, and he has maltreated others in its name. It has given him community; and it has isolated him from community almost as though he were on a desert island.

Much of this is pre-figured in the Miltonic Satan. Hell is his acknowledged realm, but, because it is Hell, he can never reconcile himself to his fall from the community of Heaven. He yearns to escape from it, but his pride dooms him to defiance of the Almighty. The fallen angels acknowledge him their Prince, and yet he is everlastingly alone in his grief and rage, the burden of which can never be lightened by being shared. Blake saw him as Desire, against the Reason that is the Miltonic Christ. In this, most of all, he is the archetype of man in Society, which can never fully assimilate the passions of its members.

Chapter 6

The Picaresque Hero

CHRISTIAN AND ROBINSON CRUSOE

I. CHRISTIAN'S PREDICAMENT

As I walked through the wilderness of this world, I lighted on a certain place, where was a Den: and I laid me down in that place to sleep: and as I slept I dreamed a Dream. I dreamed, and behold I saw a man cloathed with rags, standing in a certain place, with his face from his own House, a Book in his hand, and a great burden upon his back. I looked, and saw him open the Book, and read therein; and as he read, he wept and trembled: and not being able longer to contain, he brake out with a lamentable cry; saying, what shall I do?

THE world partakes of the Miltonic Hell – it is a wilderness; and Bunyan lies down in a 'Den' – glossed in the margin as 'The Gaol'. In the description of Christian that follows, Bunyan assimilates five biblical quotations into his text; he takes them in his stride so well that the reader, but for the marginal notes, need not be aware of their presence. It is a fair sample of his method: *Pilgrim's Progress* is a thoroughly traditional work, flowering with ease out of the Authorised Version, but from a soil compounded with medieval allegory, so that Christian recalls Everyman.

It is interesting to compare their lots. Both find themselves faced with destruction, and both discover that to escape it they must leave the world behind them. But Christian finds his warning in the Bible, which was not in the same way available to Everyman, who learns his danger by a visitation from Death. Everyman seeks help from Cousin and Kindred, but Christian, surrounded by a specific household, knows that they are in like danger – his desperation begins much sooner. Moreover Cousin and Kindred, though they despise Everyman for his pilgrimage, do not deny its reality, whereas Christian's family regard his notions as delusive: 'At this his Relations were sore amazed;

not for that they believed that what he had said to them was true, but because they thought that some frenzy distemper had got into his head: therefore, it drawing towards night, and they hoping that sleep might settle his brains, with all haste they got him to bed. . . .' Within a few lines from the solemn, visionary opening, we are in the bustle of a pack of worried women hustling a distracted man into the safest place they know. Unobtrusively, Bunyan has crossed an invisible frontier, and several centuries, into the realm of the novel.

Everyman has false friends and true friends; the false friends are outside him and the true friends are within. He has no distinct environment but rather planes of existence: he moves from a horizontal plane to a vertical one. Christian, on the other hand, has a very solid environment, and his problem is how to escape from it. His pilgrimage is an actual journey through actual places, and those he encounters, despite their allegorical names, are actual people. Faithful and Hopeful, for example, are not externalised qualities which have their real existence within Christian, as Good-Deeds represents a modicum of virtue within Everyman; they are distinct pilgrims with individual temperaments, and the second is a younger man. On the one hand they are much needed comrades, whose deficiencies Christian supplies and who supply his own; but on the other, each temperament is a loneliness, a susceptibility to special dangers with which he must often contend in unguarded solitude.

Thus Faithful does not meet Apollyon in the Valley of Humiliation though he meets Discontent and Shame whom Christian was spared; and he has 'sunshine' all through the Valley of the Shadow of Death, which was the worst of Christian's experiences. From their difference of experience, one can argue the men: Faithful the outward-turning, the extrovert, subject to temptations of the flesh and of vanity; Christian the inward-turning, the introvert, subject to self-mistrust, dread and despair. He would have perished more than once, but for the common sense of Hopeful; but Hopeful, young, adventurous, inquisitive, would have been misled by the 'gentlemanlike' Demas and his silvermine, but for Christian's warning, arising from superior self-knowledge and comparative immunity to that kind of temptation.

Truth to experience is profound in both *Everyman* and *Pilgrim's Progress*. But in *Pilgrim's Progress* there is also circumstantial actuality, and without evidence of that maze, we moderns cannot easily be persuaded that truth to experience exists. The difference places Bunyan's book well on this side of the frontier between us and the Middle Ages.

2. THREE-DIMENSIONAL ALLEGORY

Pure allegory, like the fairy tale, is commonly two-dimensional, an embodiment of a virtue or a vice moving through an abstract world peopled by such embodiments; or, as in *Everyman*, the world of the allegory is a representative figure populated by virtues and vices. In a novel, on the contrary, a character who is a nucleus of vital forces reacts to a solid world much like the reader's, and 'throws off' virtues and vices as secondary manifestations of itself. The contrast so-expressed is over-simplified, but for present purposes it will serve.

Pilgrim's Progress is between the two. Some of the figures in it are merely emblematic and drawn from traditional allegory and romance: Apollyon, Giant Despair, Mr Greatheart are of this kind, as well as the Interpreter and the denizens of his house. On the other hand the pilgrims, true and false, are, as we have already seen, less emblematic than true characters dominated by particular faults or virtues. Because a man has a quality ascribed to him so that he goes by its name, this does not necessarily mean that he has no livingness separable from that quality. The successful pilgrims have defined natures whose limitations will not allow them to achieve perfection, but on the other hand permit them each a guiding virtue which enables each progressively to surpass his limitations. In the failed pilgrims we see the opposite process; a character with some right ideas as well as wrong ones sets a barrier to his own progress by his addiction to a particular failing. Talkative is a good example. 'He was a tall man, and something more comely at a distance than at hand,' and his outlook is plausible enough to seduce

Faithful at first, though not the strenuous, exacting Christian,
so critical of himself and therefore of others.

Two indications denote this emancipation from emblem in
the *Pilgrim's Progress*. A character qualifies, or even disowns the
epithet by which he is known; for instance, By-ends declares his
to be a mere aspersion by his enemies, and in Part II Old
Honest insists that he is 'not Honest in the abstract, but Honest
is my Name, and I with my Nature may agree to what I am
called'. More important, some of the names are of uncertain
significance, such as Ready-to-halt, Muchafraid, Fearing, or
Little Faith. Such names seem to suggest 'failed' Pilgrims,
although their bearers are successful. Intrinsic merit, Bunyan
implies, is not necessarily apparent; it may be possessed in
justifying measure by a character who seems humanly in-
significant or contemptible. Faced with the River of Death,
these 'weak' characters may show unusual fineness and
serenity: 'The last words of Mr Despondency, were, Farewell
night, Welcome Day. His Daughter (Muchafraid) went
thorow the River singing, but none could understand what she
said.'

It is a frequent, though not inevitable, sign of reality in a
character that he has relationships and a milieu, which have
much to do with his nature, his behaviour, and his destiny. The
successful Pilgrim realises that he must wrench free from this
nexus just in so far as it holds him back, and Bunyan makes us
aware of it and of the varying strength of its hold. Christian's
escape is abrupt or he would not have made it; Faithful and
Hopeful, unattached men, slip away; Pliable turns back, but
is despised by his inconsistent neighbours for his inconsistency;
By-ends is tightly interwoven with his network which in reality
he values far above his salvation: '... my wife is a very virtuous
woman, the daughter of a virtuous woman; she was my Lady
Feigning's daughter, therefore she came of a very honourable
family, and is arrived to such a pitch of breeding, that she knows
how to carry it to all, even to Prince and peasant.' By-ends
values genealogy even in virtue, so that in his eyes it enhances
the virtue of a woman to be the daughter of a virtuous woman;
'honourable' is ambiguous so as to refer either to aristocracy or

to morals; and virtue comes to be replaced by breeding, so that in the end snobbery carries the day.

In the one name 'Lady Feigning', so aristocratic in its ring, so emblematic in its sense, we have a precise indication of Bunyan's transitional quality – between the medieval world painted in tempera, translucent to metaphysic, and the modern world, painted in oils, rich with corroborative circumstantial detail; between the characters of Chaucer and Shakespeare abounding with qualities for which they are conduits out of vast reservoirs of common human endowment, and a character of the new age – a knot, the pattern of whose fibres constitutes the man as he is alone in his social nexus.

3. THE CHARACTER OF A PILGRIM

'To be alone in one's social nexus' is not self-contradictory. Tied though he is at the outset into his household and environment of neighbours, Christian has no fellowship with them. The Wife of Bath enjoyed pilgrimages, partly for worldly reasons and partly because she knew that her worldliness made her a bad spiritual risk, and there is fellowship of a kind between the worldly and unworldly pilgrims to Canterbury – a town which partook of this world and the next. By Christian's day, pilgrimages are not so much out of fashion as out of consciousness, and his native town is the City of Destruction. The City is a state of mind under the dominion of Hell, as Apollyon points out – 'for all that country is mine, and I am the Prince and God of it'. Pilgrimages no longer partake both of this world and the next; they are wholly spiritual, and involve the sundering of all the old relationships and the discovery of new ones.

For Christian, this means the painful acquirement of a new nature, starting with no evident assets in his old one beyond a sense of intolerable burden. He flees from the City of Destruction, alone as becomes necessary, but he remains in Apollyon's dominions and falls into plight after plight – ridiculous as well as fearful.

That Christian is so often ridiculous is one of the important things about him. To be ridiculous is to lose face, and fear of ridicule is one of the safeguards that protect Society (the City of

Destruction, the Town of Fair Speech, Vanity Fair) against
dissolution by the Truth Seeker. Fear of ridicule ensures cohesion; willingness to risk it produces individuality. Christian
can be felt in the round because his sincerity exposes his weaknesses, and if his dedication, his doggedness, and his candour
accumulate to give him a new dignity, this is achieved in spite
of his absurdity, rather than obliterating it. This is because his
new dignity is inward while his absurdity is external, and the
terms of the allegory reveals him to us in both dimensions. It was
not, for instance, very dignified of Christian to open his Pilgrimage by falling into a bog, from which he might not have
extricated himself but for the timely intervention of Help. On
the other hand, the bog is called the Slough of Despond, and it
stands for the depression a convert falls into after the premature
elation of his conversion; moreover, Christian only earns Help
by struggling through to the further side of it. Next, still a
greenhorn in matters of spiritual wisdom, he falls a quick victim
to the quackery of Mr Worldly Wiseman, and has to be rescued
again – from under the menacing overhang of Mount Sinai; but
after all, the plausible Worldly Wiseman is good enough for
most people. His plights are commonly inward, and are none
the less real for seeming so needless to the external eye: he might
have perished in the Castle of Giant Despair had he not realised
the key of release, carried all the time in his bosom, and the
worst of his sufferings in the Valley of the Shadow of Death was
the belief that the blasphemous whisperings in his ears pro-
ceeded from his own mind, that is to say, were *willed*. Faithful's
trials were, as we have seen, mainly external, ending in martyr-
dom, but it was the destiny of Christian's temperament to travel
through the darkest places of his own spirit; despite all the trials
he had overcome and all the assurances he had received, he
would, but for Hopeful, have despaired on the verge of his
destination.

In his spiritual autobiography *Grace Abounding*, Bunyan
records his own crisis of conversion; the strength of *Pilgrim's
Progress* is the successful projection of these experiences into a
world of not only spiritual but social values. We could not understand Christian so well did we not see him in conjunction with

Pliable and Faithful, Hopeful, By-ends and Talkative, and in distinction from them. As important is to see him with Faithful in the surroundings of Vanity Fair, two incongruous figures in a setting described with causticity but yet with zestful vividness: the pilgrims are figures of fun and at the same time images of menace. They stand for truth which implies order, and the truth is life; but the Fair has its own life based on its own order. The two orders are incompatible, and the pilgrims are menacing because, though plainly ridiculous, they are immune to ridicule:

> One chanced, mocking, beholding the carriages of the men, to say unto them, What will ye buy? But they looking gravely upon him, said, We buy the Truth. At that, there was an occasion taken to despise the men the more; some mocking, some taunting, some speaking reproachfully, and some calling upon others to smite them. At last things came to an hubbub, and great stir was in the Fair, insomuch that all order was confounded.

The pilgrims are ridiculous in two ways: they are outsiders to the cities of this world, and they are outsiders to the Heavenly City. 'Outsider' of course has a different meaning in each connection: on the one hand they are refugees from the tyranny of a system of lies masquerading as truth, and on the other hand they are seekers after the truth which on its part seeks to receive them. But, as seekers, they cannot partake of the radiance that beckons them, except invisibly, so they remain odd, ungainly figures for the most part, abstaining as they must from the false appeal of the glittering world which they have rejected, and which would otherwise give them a seeming 'rightness'.

Bunyan also, of course, has rejected it, but he is artist enough to present it, and in the presentation itself to show the terms of the rejection; he knows what he is rejecting, and why, and he makes the reader know. Consider, for instance, the portrait of Madam Bubble in Part II:

HONEST: Madam Bubble? is she not a tall comely Dame, somewhat of a swarthy Complexion?
STANDFAST: Right, you hit it, she is just such a one.
HONEST: Doth she not speak very smoothly, and give you a smile at the end of every sentence?

STANDFAST: You fall right upon it again, for these are her very actions.

HONEST: Doth she not wear a great purse by her side, and is not her hand often in it, fingering her money, as if that was her Heart's Delight?

STANDFAST: 'Tis just so, had you stood by all the while, you could not more amply have set her forth before me, and have better described her features.

Madam Bubble *is* the World – that is to say, the deceitfulness of Society; Greatheart intervenes with a sermon upon her, but it does no more than add commentary to the concise, graphic depiction which Bunyan has achieved through facing out the World, instead of merely evading it by invoking its opposite.

Puritans are unpopular; Bunyan's pilgrims are in many aspects not to our taste. But taste is a barrier to experience unless we overrule it, and once we have brought ourselves to acknowledge Christian, not in his beliefs so much as in the structure of his temperament, then we find him recurring in the most unlikely regions of the field of fiction. The unlikeliness is due to the constant variation in the extent of this field; but in each variation a great novelist re-creates a pilgrimage, and, in essence, it turns out to be the same.

4. CHRISTIAN AND CRUSOE

Part I of *Pilgrim's Progress* was published in 1678; the first part of *Robinson Crusoe* came out in 1719. Some forty years apart in time, how near and how far are they in spirit? It is not easy to tabulate their differences and resemblances, for often where they seem most alike they disclose their greatest contrasts, and where they seem to have least in common they disclose their greatest community.

Their predicaments have this in common: both are lonely men, and their loneliness – in Christian from the start and in Crusoe later on – is involved with a sense of sin. To both, therefore, other people are peculiarly important; but not just any people. A sharp distinction is made by each between those with whom he can share community, and those with whom no community is possible, at least of the kind that either pilgrim –

for as we shall see Crusoe is also a pilgrim – finds in his nature the compulsion to build.

Both men embark on journeys, and both abandon their families. However, Christian's journey is a spiritual one, and his desertion is only apparent, for he shows his family the way and in Part II they follow him; whereas Crusoe really forsakes his parents to go on a physical journey, and never sees them again. Yet allegory and straight narrative have a wilful way of converging when they seem to diverge from their very starting points: Crusoe's journeys were literal, but I shall try to show that none the less they had spiritual meaning; Christian's journey was allegorical, but it is literally presented, and has a destination as well as a destiny. In one sense their destinations are similar, for both men are travelling home. Christian, when he crosses the River of Death, comes home for the first time. Crusoe, when he comes home for his last time, is really achieving his first arrival there, for home is where one's spirit is settled, and Crusoe only settles when the agony of his wanderlust is quenched by old age. Settlement resulting from exhaustion, admittedly, cannot be final in a spiritual meaning, and the last sentence of the book seems to show that he is aware of Christian's journey still to come: 'And here I resolved to prepare for a longer journey than all these, having lived a life of infinite variety seventy two years, and learned sufficiently to know the value of retirement, and the blessing of ending our days in peace.' Yet do these lines really signpost Christian's road? The tone is not at all of Christian's anguish, but on the contrary of a man well contented with what he has found in this City of Destruction. He mentions 'variety', and we may add, plenty of money. At the obvious level, it is easy to contrast Christian's spiritual singleness with Crusoe's underlying worldliness. We must do justice to this contrast, but when we have done it, we shall see that once again it is more apparent than real, that Crusoe has tried to prove something, and in proving it has himself undergone a kind of spiritual probation.

Christian undertakes his journey under the most peremptory injunction; only twice does he wander from his prescribed path, and then under misapprehension. Crusoe sets out against the injunction of his respectable father; he flees, not from any City of Destruction, but from the tedium of 'the upper station of low life'. Christian wants nothing from this world, and in theory, but in that only, Crusoe agrees with him; in practice he likes wealth, and achieves it. When, for instance, he finds money on the wreck, he first of all subjects it to a pious diatribe, and then, 'upon second thoughts', prudently pockets it. In human beings, it is the economic virtues and advantages that he cares for. On his desert island it is not a woman he desires as company but a devoted slave, whom he finds in Friday; and the character he reveres most in the entire narrative is the Portuguese who scrupulously guards Crusoe's Brazilian estates all the many years he has been missing and might have been presumed dead. The colony he establishes on the island is strictly a godless one – a purely economic community, as the French priest points out to him. As a final example of this apparently heartless materialism, we have the unpleasant instance of Crusoe's faithful Moroccan boy Xury whom he sells to a sea-captain, without remorse, though, it is true, not without some qualms. There are no signs on Crusoe's, or his author's, part that there is any incongruity between the confessed sinfulness of Crusoe's wanderlust and the prosperity which it brings and which he so much appreciates. At most, there is the recurrent stern reminder that his good fortune is countenanced by the mercy of Providence, and, like any other debt, should be acknowledged accordingly. In fact, Crusoe's relationship with his Maker is itself an economic one: the sort of relationship that one might have with a powerful Patron, whose boundless generosity cannot be repaid in kind, but who none the less expects a return in gratitude and adulation.

Such is a sketch of the case against Crusoe. It could be amplified with similar detail, but it is already strong. Yet it is not even the more important part of the whole truth.

First of all, some of the evidence, when inspected in accordance with the Puritan lights of Crusoe and his author, is not so damning as it seems by other lights. It is a condition of the sale of Xury, for example, that he shall be granted his freedom when he grows up provided that he adopts Christianity. At first sight, this seems to make the deal even worse: Xury is not merely being sold by Crusoe who had no real proprietary rights over him, but he is to be blackmailed into abandoning his native Moslem faith as well. Defoe, on the other hand, would suppose that Crusoe was on the contrary performing Xury a double service, by securing simultaneously his freedom and enlightenment. Again, Defoe might be surprised at the idea that there is any incongruity in Crusoe prospering from voyages whose outset, at least, he himself confesses to derive from a sinful impulse. He would say that God is merciful even to a sinner, and that we miss the point if we do not see that just this is the theme of the book; that Crusoe, in rejoicing over his good fortune, is rejoicing also in God's goodness to him.

This sort of defence, however, is uninspiringly negative, and no amount of apology will make Crusoe seem a very good Christian by Bunyan's standards. His religious exercises and reflections are carried on separately from his practical living, except when the two sides are shocked into mutual engagement, especially by some kind of danger, and then only during the crisis. In principle, he recognises that he owes his constant escapes from danger to God, but he also provides natural explanations to himself, so that the role of God becomes, for the reader, somewhat hypothetical. Mere absence of religion in another man ceases to shock him, except when his attention is drawn to it. On the other hand, besides this unpuritan laxity, he also shows an unpuritan liberality; his reverence for the economic virtues – such as industry, good faith, endurance, loyalty – also shows itself as a rational respect for people as social beings, whatever their nationhood or faith. It is the Spaniards on his island who are the exemplary settlers, and the English whose violence and irresponsibility have to be subdued. But this liberality extends beyond the merely social relationships: he allows himself to be humbled by the French Catholic priest in regard to the irreligion of his colony, and accepts his guidance. If, except in crises, less devout, Crusoe is easier to live with than Christian had been; intensity of feeling and poetry are gone, or are going, but reason and breadth of experience have taken their place.

This is a very usual view to take of Robinson Crusoe; yet it will not quite do. It leaves out the element of savagery and violence in the book and the way in which it is related to other elements – order, Crusoe's self, and Providence. In particular, one or two episodes seem to show that Crusoe was, after all, very deeply concerned with Providence, though not in the way that Christian was.

In the most famous sequence, Crusoe creates order out of a wilderness; he establishes a society of himself and a few animals. This cosy world – but to his credit it is not its cosiness that he esteems, but simply its order – is menaced by the cannibals with their abandoned, horrible rites. Their savagery rouses in Crusoe a corresponding savagery, but he is sufficiently civilised – that is to say, conscious enough – to understand that an un-provoked attack on them on his part would itself be a crime in the eyes of Providence, who had seen fit to leave them undis-turbed in their practices. When this peril is survived, and the colony, composed of rescued seafarers, is established, the island is afflicted with a new savagery in the lawlessness of the English sailors led by Atkins. The two island sequences are the main features of the two parts of the book, whose principal secondary features are Crusoe's capture by Moslem pirates in the first part, and his marooning and perilous overland return across Asia, in the second. The first part opens with Crusoe's own act of law-lessness in running away to sea from the order and placidity of his home; the second part ends with the extraordinary episode of the destruction of the idol Cham Chi-Thaungu in Eastern Russia:

In a village . . . I had the curiosity to go and see their way of living, which is most brutish and insufferable: they had, I suppose, a great sacrifice that day; for there stood out, upon an old stump of a tree, an idol, made of wood, frightful as the devil; at least, as anything we can think of to represent the devil can be made: it had a head not so much as resembling any creature that the world ever saw; ears as big as goats' horns, and as high; eyes as big as a crown piece; a nose like a crooked ram's horn, and a mouth extended four-cornered, like that of a lion, with horrible teeth, hooked like a parrot's under bill: it was dressed up in the filthiest manner that you could suppose: its upper garment was of sheepskins, with the wool outward: a great Tartar bonnet on the head, with two horns growing through it: it was about eight feet high, yet had no feet or legs, nor any other proportion of parts.

Two words here, 'curiosity', 'insufferable', show two sides of Crusoe's nature: the overt one that everyone knows, and the hidden, which appears indirectly, but gives his adventures their depth and meaning. Overtly we have Crusoe who is the opposite to Christian; Crusoe the outward-turning man occupied always with the practical demands of a situation: how to escape from slavery, how to survive on a desert island, how to transform a savage into a reliable servant, how to get back to England across Asia and Europe, how to destroy an idol. In all these activities he gives an impression of truthfulness to external event, and it is his perpetual preoccupation with it, his endless confidence in his own resourcefulness, which gives him the consistency that we find so convincing and has made him famous. His curiosity drives him to ceaseless exploration, experimentation, construction and organisation; it makes him patient with and tolerant of alien people and their ways of life.

But his patience and tolerance have limits, as do his courage and resolution. When he is desperately sea-sick, overcome with terror, alone and overwhelmed by fever, it is natural that he should then recall his actual weakness and real dependence on a merciful Providence. But Providence is more than merely merciful; it is the underlying guarantee of order in the Universe, the enabling force behind civilisation. Without faith in Providence, civilisation becomes a pretentious sham, as he finds it in China, or men are abandoned to hideous barbarities like those of the cannibals. Much of the time he seems to take Providence for granted, but his reliance on it is consistent and profound, and the worship of an opposite principle such as Cham Chi-Thaungu is 'insufferable'. It has to be destroyed before the eyes of its priests – even at immense risk to Crusoe's own life and to the lives of the entire caravan of merchants with which he is travelling – because he has to prove that no opposite principle to Providence can contend against it. The entire book is a heroic saga of a single man, backed by Providence, maintaining order against violence, in nature and in man, and the destruction of the idol is its fitting climax.

What then is the silence of life? And, how is it afflicting, while a man has the voice of his soul to speak to God, and to himself?

This is Crusoe in the little read Part III – 'The Serious Reflections' – where he also says: '. . . I can affirm, that I enjoy much more solitude in the middle of the greatest collection of mankind in the world, I mean, at London, while I am writing this, than ever I could say I enjoy'd in eight and twenty years confinement to a desolate island.'

5. THE ORIGIN OF LONELINESS

Satan, Christian, Crusoe: they are a very incongruous trio to draw together, and very distinct were the aims of their creators in presenting them. Yet they have in common that all three are outcasts, seekers, wanderers: Satan, the outcast from Heaven, seeking a new Heaven in his own sufficiency, wandering between Hell and Earth; Christian performing the Journey in reverse, an outcast from the City of Destruction, seeking the Heavenly City, wandering along the borders of Hell; Crusoe, the outcast from the security he could not take for granted, seeking to rebuild and rediscover it, wandering through a universe of dangers as though unconsciously testing its foundation in divine assurance.

The three creations were published within just over half a century; thereafter, their impulses and predicaments – their need to escape, their urge to find, their sense of isolation – recur in that image of man which we call imaginative fiction. Seeking and wandering had of course long been themes of literature; isolation is the crisis through which Everyman and Sir Gawayne both pass. But loneliness is henceforth to be accepted as the basic human condition, and that is new. The newness arises with a new conviction, consciously or unconsciously held, that God is no longer imminent, but at best distant and inscrutable. So man seeks man, sometimes in and through, sometimes against and in spite of, Society.

Part 3

Character and Society

Chapter 7

The Heroine Victim 1
EMMA WOODHOUSE OF *EMMA*
CATHERINE EARNSHAW OF *WUTHERING HEIGHTS*

I. SOCIETY AS CONFINEMENT

Emma Woodhouse, handsome, clever, and rich, with a comfortable home and happy disposition, seemed to unite some of the blessings of existence; and had lived nearly twenty-one years in the world with very little to distress or vex her.

Emma was published in 1816. Earthly lots and destinies were much what they had been, but they had come to possess illusory finality and power of definition. In this opening sentence we are shown a character who 'seems', at her very outset, to have arrived. She is what she needs to be, and has what is to be desired. Emma has no defects which Society would call defects, nor lacks anything that Society would regard as worth regretting. Yet we are told that she '*Seemed* to unite *some* of the blessings . . .', and out of the germs of doubt in those two words, the whole novel consistently unfurls.

Emma's good fortune turns out to be golden confinement and double delusion: confinement, because its perfection precludes the idea of enlargement; delusion, because not only does it seem to render needless any effort by Emma on her own behalf, but it seems to confer the right, almost the duty, to make efforts on the behalf of others. So, her own destiny ready moulded to such advantage, Emma takes it upon herself to mould that of another.

For doing this she has the advantages of social position, natural kindness, and quick intelligence; her obvious disadvantage is her youthful inexperience of life and lack of self-knowledge – negative faults made lethal by her perfect self-confidence, based on the unquestioning deference which all her relations and friends, except Knightley, consider her due. To these disqualifications must be added another which is yet more serious inasmuch as it is so far from being obvious to her that it may be missed even by the reader, who is being 'shown the cards': she makes a common but basic confusion between literature and life.

The relationship of literature to life, especially the intrusion of literature into life and the way in which experience of the imagination can deteriorate into mere imaginary experience, are constituents of at least four of Jane Austen's six novels. In *Northanger Abbey* Catherine Morland tries to live the romance of a gothic romance and becomes entangled in real-life confusions for which she is not prepared; in *Sense and Sensibility* Marianne Dashwood, priding herself in her 'sensibility', turns her disappointment in love into a romantic catastrophe, leaving her sister – mere 'sense' – to contend with its disruptive effects on private life while she has her private sorrow to contend with as well. In *Mansfield Park* a group of young people involve their precarious and little understood personal relationships with amateur theatricals and precipitate disaster.

Emma, inexperienced in human nature, ignorant equally of the facts in other people's lives and of her own deeper feelings, tries to compose a real-life romantic novel centred on Harriet Smith, becomes a willing but unwitting puppet in a real-life farce contrived by Frank Churchill, tries to include him as a character in her novel, and finds in the end that she is on the point of bringing about a triple tragedy – that of Harriet Smith, of Jane Fairfax, and of herself.

Her initial mistake is to suppose that a person such as herself, with every external advantage, is fitted to operate other people's lives as an author operates those of his characters. Her second great error is not to perceive the interconnection between what is social and what is personal, and that in arriving at social as well as personal judgements, we commonly do no more than project our prejudices and predilections, often hidden from ourselves. She adopts Harriet Smith, who is 'the natural daughter of somebody', because Harriet's prettiness makes her a promising investment, and because her submissiveness makes her amenable to Emma's own strong will. Emma, however, chooses to see the prettiness and the submissiveness as evidences

of natural refinement and aristocratic parentage, and a suitable
pretext for romance. The fact that submissiveness may equally
show weakness of mind and mediocrity of personality does not
occur to her because of its inconvenience. Similarly, she arrives
at conclusions convenient to herself about Robert Martin, the
modest farmer whose engagement to Harriet she succeeds in
preventing, and of the vicar, Mr Elton, whose engagement to
Harriet she tries to bring about, but who, to her intense
indignation, chooses instead to propose to herself:

She thought nothing of his attachment, and was insulted by his
hopes. He wanted to marry well, and having the arrogance to raise
his eyes to her, pretended to be in love; but she was perfectly at
ease as to his not suffering any disappointment that need be cared
for. There had been no real affection either in his language or
manners. Sighs and fine words had been given in abundance; but
she could hardly devise any set of expressions, or fancy any tone of
voice, less allied with real love. She need not trouble herself to pity
him. He only wanted to aggrandize and enrich himself. . . .

All this is perfectly true: Elton's proposal to Emma is heartless.
Yet, such is her ignorance of the disposition of her own heart,
that she does not see how all her reflections about Elton's
motives towards herself apply equally to her own motives on
behalf of Harriet. She has been equally heartless in breaking the
relationship between Harriet and Robert Martin; as much as
the Vicar for himself has she 'only wanted' aggrandisement and
enrichment for Harriet. She cannot even be excused on the
ground that at least she wants these things for another, for it is
evident that she is trying to live through Harriet the romance
which she believes to be denied to herself, owing to the ready-
made good fortune which makes her own existence so perfect.

When Harriet remonstrates with her for her willingness to
become an old maid, she has her answer ready, and it is an
answer that reveals so much about Emma that it constitutes a
key passage in the book:

'I shall not be a poor old maid; and it is poverty only which
makes celibacy contemptible to a generous public! A single
woman, with a very narrow income, must be a ridiculous disagreeable old maid! . . . And the distinction is not quite so much against

CHARACTER IN ENGLISH LITERATURE

the candour and common sense of the world as appears at first; for a very narrow income has a tendency to contract the mind, and sour the temper. . . . This does not apply, however, to Miss Bates; she is only too good-natured and too silly to suit me; but in general, she is very much to the taste of everybody, though single and though poor. Poverty certainly has not contracted her mind: I really believe, if she had only a shilling in the world, she would be very likely to give away sixpence of it; and nobody is afraid of her: that is a great charm.'

'Dear me! but what shall you do? How shall you employ yourself when you grow old?'

'If I know myself, Harriet, mine is an active, busy mind, with a great many independent resources; and I do not perceive why I shall be more in want of employment at forty or fifty than at one-and-twenty. Women's usual occupations of eye, and hand and mind, will be as open to me then as they are now, or with no important variation. If I draw less, I shall read more; If I give up music, I shall take to carpet-work. And as for objects of interest, objects for the affections, which is in truth the great point of inferiority, the want of which is really the great evil to be avoided in *not* marrying, I shall be very well off, with all the children of a sister I love so much to care about. There will be enough of them in all probability, to supply every sort of sensation that declining life can need. There will be enough for every hope and every fear; and though my attachment to none can equal that of a parent, it suits my ideas of comfort better than what is warmer and blinder. My nephews and nieces! – I shall often have a niece with me.'

Emma contrasts her prospective self to Miss Bates. What she says about old maids and social attitudes to them shows genuine acuteness; but it strikes one that this blooming, arrogant, lively-minded girl will find it hard to grow into such a happy and beloved old maid as that simple-minded but generous and zestful old lady, so full with interest in the smallest details of her narrow life that she can never complete a sentence about any of them. Emma will always have 'occupations' for her talents, but the word is dreadful in its context, suggesting as it does that her life will be so much empty space to be carefully and precisely filled. And what of the voids that no 'Occupation' can supply? She will have nephews and nieces. One remembers that diffident sister and devoted mother, Isabella, who would find it so hard to resist the masterful, auntly incursions, and so hard not to resent them, and one ponders her husband – strong-minded, assertive, a doting father; one contemplates his rage. Emma playing with the lives of her hephews and nieces, as she is at this moment playing with the life of Harriet, is no engaging prospect. Miss Bates bores everyone with her niece, Jane Fairfax, but Miss Bates is to Jane an authentic refuge, not the moulder of fate that Emma would become.

It is part of Jane Austen's art of character creation that she erects, beside the central characters, others which provide analogy and satirical contrast to them. Miss Bates is such an oblique commentary: she does no harm and affords far more innocent pleasure to those whom she bores than Emma is likely to do to those whom she interests. A still severer commentary is the character of Mrs Elton, whom Mr Elton marries after his rebuff by Emma. Mrs Elton is vulgar, stupid and affected, whereas Emma is refined, intelligent and natural, and observes the Vicar's new wife with horrified wonderment; but she does not observe that Mrs Elton is, in her outlook and conduct, a brutal caricature of herself. Emma is quietly satisfied to be the queen of local society, but Mrs Elton arrogates to herself that position; Emma allows social distinctions to confuse her personal judgements, but Mrs Elton judges by social distinctions alone; Emma supposes that she can take over a simple, inexperienced girl and mould her life for her; but Mrs Elton supposes that her own patronage is required by Jane Fairfax, observing that she is diffident and poor, and not being capable of observing that she is reserved, proud, cultivated and talented; in short in every personal way the superior not only of herself but also of Emma, whom alone Mrs Elton regards as her equal.

Jane Fairfax is the third of the characters who act as a foil for Emma's virtues and failings. Her personal superiority to Emma is masked by her poverty, and emphasises the shallowness and unconscious cruelty of Emma's standards, and of all standards that arise from merely social discrimination. She is beautiful, and artistic to the extent of exposing Emma as a dabbler; but her poverty means that her engagement to Frank

Churchill must remain a secret during the lifetime of his aunt, for fear of losing the legacy which, socially speaking, is necessary to their marriage. Churchill is not at all embarrassed, but enjoys cloaking the secret by a flirtation with Emma, and encouraging Emma's piqued, romantic speculations about Jane's circumstances. The engagement becomes precarious, and Jane's acceptance of a post as governess under Mrs Elton's patronage is narrowly averted. Emma's shrewd but flippant-toned remarks on poor old maids bear cruelly on Jane's situation. The double image of Emma as the interfering, complacent, empty-lived aunt, and Jane as the faded, diffident, impecunious governess, which at one point seems to be their likely fates, is also a tragic image of human waste, before which only a Mrs Elton could retain oblivious satisfaction.

Insensibility breeds unreality: Harriet, having been encouraged to aspire to Mr Elton, is now encouraged by Emma to aspire still further: Frank Churchill rescues her from an unpleasant encounter with some gipsies and the incident titillates Emma's imagination – it savours so well of a romantic novel. It is here, however, that she makes her climactic and most ridiculous mistake; romance and discretion alike dictate that no names should be mentioned in their discussions, with the result that while Emma supposes Harriet to be excited into gratitude and devotion to Frank on account of the gipsies, Harriet is really being drawn into love with Knightley on account of a very different service – Knightley has saved her vanity by inviting her to dance when she is left stranded at a ball. Emma believes that she knows Harriet's whole heart, but she knows it so little that she doesn't realise how little a serious embarrassment with gipsies weighs, for this young girl, against the humiliation of being left a wallflower. Sedulously, she encourages Harriet's hopes, until the Churchhill-Fairfax engagement becomes public, and the moment of truth breaks.

Harriet was standing at one of the windows. Emma turned round to look at her in consternation, and hastily said:

'Have you any idea of Mr Knightley's returning your affection?'

'Yes,' replied Harriet modestly, but not fearfully; 'I must say that I have.'

Emma's eyes were instantly withdrawn; and she sat silently meditating, in a fixed attitude, for a few minutes. A few minutes were sufficient for making her acquainted with her own heart. A mind like hers, once opening to suspicion, made rapid progress. She touched – she admitted – she acknowledged the whole truth. Why was it so much worse that Harriet should be in love with Mr Knightley, than with Frank Churchill? Why was the evil so dreadfully increased by Harriet's having some hope of return? It darted through her, with the speed of an arrow, that Mr Knightley must marry no one but herself!

This is the first time that Emma, intelligent as she is, sees and understands her own feelings, and the insight comes with the realisation that in seeking to contrive Harriet's fortune she has succeeded in contriving a scaffold for the destruction of her own happiness.

All the tragedies are averted: Emma marries Knightley; Jane marries Churchill; Harriet is taken back by Robert Martin. Jane Austen is after all, a writer of comedies. Comedies of depth, however, always provide a glimpse of the tragic alternative, and in every one of her novels this looms up before it is made to fade away. The heroines all have double standards, and usually employ them consciously: Society demands its due of deference; yet personal integrity has to be maintained. So placid, easy and secure is the surface lot of a Jane Austen heroine, that many people take her novels as sedatives; yet the heroines are tight-rope walkers, and Emma is a blindfolded one, whose bandage is torn from her eyes only just in time.

On a tightrope, every step is crucial, and every word is made to count by this novelist. The minuteness of treatment, the closeness of scrutiny that results, exceeds anything that we have so far studied, and the interplay of personal and social attitudes and responses makes for a corresponding richness of character-tone. There is no unnatural contrast between the two; it is not that the personal is white and the social black; indeed, at the end of the book, the social criteria happen to be endorsed. Thus, it is conventionally suitable for Emma, the first lady of Highbury, to marry Knightley, the first gentleman; Harriet turns out to be the daughter of a tradesman and is after all not at all too good for Robert Martin; Churchill has rich maternal relations, but he is the modest Mr Weston's son for whom Jane is by no means too low. Does Jane Austen, then, after all, connive at these merely external criteria? Not at all; for what happens to be socially 'right' is achieved notwithstanding on the personal ground, and even in the teeth of what the 'Society-minded' – Emma, Mrs Elton, the invisible but powerful Mrs Churchill – try to impose. Emma is not shown to be altogether wrong in attaching value to social distinctions, for in her society they were generally involved in personal identities. She is, however, altogether wrong in failing to put the personal values first, allowing the social ones to take care of themselves – wrong both on the personal and the social counts. She is wrong not because she is superficial, stupid, or heartless, but because her social position gives her a false perspective both of personal values and of her own nature. The parable of the camel and the needle's eye applies to her; but so does Blake's proverb: 'If a fool should persist in his folly, he would grow wise.' Of the three marriages in prospect at the end of the novel, only that of Emma and Knightley has assurance of happiness, for they alone have justly assorted the personal and the social categories.

2. SATAN AGAINST SOCIETY

While enjoying a month of fine weather at the sea-coast, I was thrown into the company of a most fascinating creature: a real goddess in my eyes, as long as she took no notice of me. I 'never told my love' vocally; still, if looks have language, the merest idiot might have guessed I was over head and ears: she understood me at last, and looked a return – the sweetest of all imaginable looks. And what did I do? I confess it with shame – shrunk icily into myself, like a snail; at every glance retired colder and farther; till finally the poor innocent was led to doubt her senses, and, overwhelmed with confusion at her supposed mistake, persuaded her mamma to decamp. By this curious turn of disposition I have gained the reputation of deliberate heartlessness; how undeserved, I alone can appreciate.

Wuthering Heights is a novel about sexual passion, and the central relationship in it is so extraordinary that the novelist sets it in the perspective of more familiar forms of the passion so that the reader may adjust himself to it the more truly. Emily Brontë also tells the story through a number of narrators; these are witnesses of the events and bear characters such as the reader is likely to trust, inasmuch as they are familiar types of human being, so that what they record is the more credible for surviving their incredulity; at the same time, by the way in which they record it, they expose the shallowness of ordinary human feeling such as their own, and such as is likely to be the reader's.

These narrators are three. We have Lockwood, who is the subject of the anecdote quoted above; he is the dandy who supposes himself sensitive because, being weak in the capacity to feel very strongly himself, he is frightened by strong, true, direct emotion on the part of others. He is the direct witness in the opening and the closing chapters, but for the main narrative he is merely the audience for Nelly Dean. Nelly is a housekeeper, peasant-born but self-educated, strong minded, and the possessor of much practical sense. Finally, there is Isabella Linton. She begins as a sentimental, romantic young lady who conceives a Byronic passion for the central character, Heathcliff, and tells her story after he has knocked the romance out of her. This system of narrators is like a contrivance of lenses: they correct one another, and enable us to focus all the better because we understand their limitations. Novelists often try for invisibility, but few have attained it so successfully as Emily Brontë.

The styles of sexual emotion in the novel are no fewer than five, two of which have already been mentioned. Lockwood's anecdote shows the most familiar of all: the flirtation, of which alone he is capable. Lockwood plays no role except that of witness and auditor, and apart from providing a motive for his retirement to a solitary spot, the main functions of the incident seem to be to 'place' him in these capacities, and to start the reader off in shallow water. Isabella's infatuation is by its nature immature, and the familiar pathos of it emphasises Heathcliff's frenetic cruelty in crushing it so ruthlessly. It also serves to warn the reader against supposing that the Catherine-Heathcliff affair is anything of the kind. It is this affair that forms the central, most extraordinary relationship in the book, but its extraordinariness is only intelligible by juxtaposing it with that between Edgar Linton and Catherine, which precedes it, and that between Catherine Linton and Hareton Earnshaw with which the story ends. This last is the only one that is truly blessed: a union of pure love replacing hate and uncontaminated by ulterior influences even of the most harmless. The marriage between Catherine Earnshaw and Edgar Linton, on the other hand, is the normal union: socially suitable, entered upon partly for convenience, but yet with a large constituent of mutual tenderness. In the following dialogue, Catherine is trying to express to Nelly her feeling of uneasiness about her engagement to Edgar; Nelly probes, sure that such uneasiness must mean disingenuousness of feeling somewhere:

'Why do you love him, Miss Cathy?'
'Nonsense, I do – that's sufficient.'
'By no means; you must say why?'
'Well, because he is handsome, and pleasant to be with.'
'Bad!' was my commentary.
'And because he is young and cheerful.'
'Bad still.'
'And because he loves me.'
'Indifferent, coming there.'
'And he will be rich, and I shall be the greatest woman of the neighbourhood, and I shall be proud of having such a husband.'
'Worst of all. And now, say how you love him?'
'As everybody loves – You're silly, Nelly.'
'Not at all – Answer.'
'I love the ground under his feet, and the air over his head, and everything he touches, and every word he says. I love all his looks, and all his actions, and him entirely and altogether. There now!'
'And why?'

At this point, Catherine quite loses patience, and small wonder, for she is perfectly sincere, and on the usual terms of fiction or real life her love is indeed irreproachable. Not surprisingly, then, Nelly does not understand Catherine when she at last gets to the ground of her misgiving, which she expresses through a dream that she has had. She has dreamt that she is in heaven:

'. . . I was only going to say that heaven did not seem to be my home; and I broke my heart with weeping to come back to earth; and the angels were so angry that they flung me out into the middle of the heath on the top of Wuthering Heights; where I woke sobbing for joy. That will do to explain my secret. . . . I've no more business to marry Edgar Linton than I have to be in heaven; and if the wicked man in there had not brought Heathcliff so low, I shouldn't have thought of it. It would degrade me to marry Heathcliff now; so he shall never know how I love him: and that, not because he's handsome Nelly, but because he's more myself than I am. Whatever my souls are made of, his and mine are the same; and Linton's is as different as a moonbeam from lightning, or frost from fire.'

Her intention is to raise Heathcliff with Edgar's money, and 'the wicked man in there' who has 'brought Heathcliff so low' is her half-brother Hindley. But to understand this and the nature of Catherine's feeling, one needs to know more of Heathcliff and of how he came into the Earnshaw household.

He was brought to the Heights by Catherine's father – some years before the above dialogue – after a journey to Liverpool.

'See here, wife! I was never so beaten with anything in my life: but you must e'en take it as a gift from God; though it's as dark almost as if it came from the devil.'

We crowded round, and over Miss Cathy's head, I had a peep at a dirty, ragged, black-haired child; big enough both to walk and talk: indeed its face looked older than Catherine's; yet, when it was set on its feet, it only stared round, and repeated over and over again some gibberish, that nobody could understand. I was frightened, and Mrs Earnshaw was ready to fling it out of doors: she did fly up, asking how he could fashion to bring that gipsy brat into the house, when they had their own bairns to feed and fend for? What he meant to do with it, and whether he were mad? The master tried to explain the matter . . . and all that I could make out . . . was a tale of his seeing it starving, and houseless, and as good as dumb, in the streets of Liverpool; where he picked it up and enquired for its owner. Not a soul knew to whom it belonged, he said; and his money and time being both limited, he thought it better to take it home with him at once, than run into vain expenses there: because he was determined he would not leave it as he found it.

Well, the conclusion was that my mistress grumbled herself calm; and Mr Earnshaw told me to wash it, and give it clean things, and let it sleep with the children.

So Heathcliff – this is his only name, and given to him by Mr Earnshaw – is virtually taken out of the jungle, but an urban jungle, for he is in Society but not of it from the start. The jungle is the more unnatural for being urban, but not the less savage: Heathcliff is as much animal as child, and the pronoun used in reference to him is 'it'. He is brought to Wuthering Heights, which represents a frontier post of civilisation, for it is an ancient farm set among the moors. In consequence, though the Earnshaws are a proud family, life among them is simple, as it commonly is among frontiersmen of the wilderness: they have no time for refinements; a democracy reigns among masters and servants, so that the latter are also friends and confidants, living with the former and accustomed to unusual freedom speech; the children run wild on the moors. As a community, it is in some ways more open and in others more exclusive than communities farther within the frontier, such as Thrushcross Grange where the Lintons live: it is open to the wild and to simple ways of life, but it is jealously close in its pattern of relationships within itself. Thus, Heathcliff can be received, but he is not assimilated. Old Earnshaw dotes on him as a man only dotes on his pets, but he is hated with jealous fury by the elder child, Hindley, and disliked and distrusted as an intruder by all the rest of the family except Catherine. With her, Heathcliff develops a close fellowship, integrated by the moors. In the house he is only more and more the hated and despised alien, but the moors and Catherine give him this perfect bond, assuming all other bonds which in the 'social' being are distributed amongst family, friends, habits, and environment.

Though Heathcliff is the most extraordinary character in the book it is Catherine Earnshaw who is its structural centre, for she alone is in tension among its various forces. Drawn out of the Earnshaw orbit in one direction by Heathcliff, she is also attracted in another by the Lintons: enlargement in civilisation is set over against enlargement in wild nature. She tries, as we

THE HEROINE VICTIM 1

THE HEROINE VICTIM 1

have seen, to choose both, but Heathcliff runs away. Catherine becomes Edgar Linton's wife, and a fine lady.

I got Miss Catherine and myself to Thrushcross Grange; and to my agreeable disappointment, she behaved infinitely better than I dared to expect. She seemed almost over-fond of Mr Linton; and even to his sister she showed plenty of affection. They were both very attentive to her comfort, certainly. It was not the thorn bending to the honeysuckles, but the honeysuckles embracing the thorn. There were no mutual concessions; one stood erect, and the others yielded: and who *can* be ill-natured and bad-tempered when they encounter neither opposition nor indifference? I observed that Mr Edgar had a deep-rooted fear of ruffling her humour. He concealed it from her; but if ever he heard me answer sharply, or saw any other servant grow cloudy at some imperious order of hers, he would show his trouble by a frown of displeasure that never darkened on his own account. . . . Catherine had seasons of gloom and silence now and then: they were respected with sympathising silence by her husband, who ascribed them to an alteration in her constitution, produced by her perilous illness; as she was never subject to depression of spirits before. . . . I believe I may assert that they were really in possession of deep and growing happiness.

What does a wild animal lose by being tamed? Catherine's capacity for happiness is increased, but her personality is reduced. Her enlargement into civilisation is a reduction to happiness; but, as Nelly goes on to say, 'It ended.' For Heathcliff returns. From the outset, a pariah to Society, he comes back to find Catherine, not, certainly, his enemy, but so to speak an enemy captive. His passion for her is as great, and he is ruthless towards everyone, particularly Edgar, who stands between them, and he exploits Isabella's infatuation to marry her and use her for his own ends. He ruins Hindley by exploiting his addiction to gambling and drink, and perhaps murders him. Catherine's agony leads to a death in childbirth, and she is later followed by her anguished husband.

He is left, eventually, with only the younger generation: Linton Heathcliff, his own son by Isabella and a Linton by character; Catherine's daughter, who takes after her mother; and Hindley's son, Hareton. One might suppose that his rage

I   129

would by this time have exhausted itself, but his love for Catherine is as great for her dead as when she was living; the difference is that it can now only be expressed through hatred – through the systematic destruction of the two families that frustrated it. He forces a marriage of mutual dislike between his own son, Linton Heathcliff, and Catherine's daughter, Catherine Linton, in order to gain control over both properties; he seeks to brutalise Hareton as Hareton's father had sought to brutalise himself.

The doubt which must strike the reader is whether the character of Heathcliff is 'credible'. Several answers can be made, and one arises from his ultimate failure to destroy Hareton and Catherine. His son, Linton, a sickly youth for whom he has no feeling except contempt, dies not long after his marriage to the young Catherine; but Hareton resists sheer brutalisation. He is a boor, but he retains dignity, and this for the unexpected reason that, in trying to reduce him into an image of what he has himself been, Heathcliff is not creating a brute. A brutal and brutalised maniac is much what Heathcliff's own persecutor, Hindley, became, but what Heathcliff himself has never been; if he had, he would be incredible on the grounds that he could not have made himself rich during his three years absence from the Heights, and he could not thereafter have completed his plans of vengeance as far as he did. Heathcliff is demonic – and as to the credibility of this, answers have to be made of a different kind – but his passion is not degraded nor degrading, and his ferocity is finely tempered, ruthless when he sees his purpose, but never wasting itself in senseless violence. The result is that instead of loathing and fearing his persecutor, Hareton becomes, as Heathcliff himself says, 'damnably fond' of him, and seeks to emulate him. Catherine Linton, used to the Linton education and refinement, at first despises him, and he feels humiliated by her; but the Earnshaw side is dominant in her, while he is far from being without finer potentialities. So they draw gradually together: 'They lifted their eyes together, to encounter Mr Heathcliff: perhaps you have never remarked that their eyes are precisely similar, and they are those of Catherine Earnshaw . . . I suppose this resemblance disarmed

Mr Heathcliff. . . .' When his enemies look at him with Catherine's eyes, Heathcliff begins to relax his hold on his hatred, and so on life; he begins his strange, haunted, or enchanted, drift towards the only union with her that was ever possible.

A second answer to doubts as to Heathcliff's credibility might be a challenge to the reader's notions of credibility itself. In a novel, we have come to expect a character to be real in terms of social definition, what Lawrence was later to call 'the social ego'. Even our idea of an anti-social man is such a man on social terms: a negative is defined by the positive it denies. Heathcliff, however, is positive; he is the man imbued with natural force, all his life long at war with the social force that excludes – not him, but the human passion which absorbs his titanism. Such a conception is perhaps only possible in the state of society that the novel pictures, and such as existed in the northern England of Emily Brontë's time. She shows us not one world capable of producing one whole way of life, but two, and two more by implication. There is the modern wilderness of the Liverpool slums, where human life is reduced to the level of struggling vermin; there is the immemorial wilderness of the moors in their primitive violence; there is Wuthering Heights, representative of an old human order, already anachronistic in that its daughters will marry into the new order of Thrushcross Grange, with which Jane Austen might have been on visiting terms. Without the desolation of the slums, Heathcliff might never have been transported to the Heights, nor would he have been so alien there; without the liberation and constrictions of Wuthering Heights and the moors, Catherine and he would not have achieved the freedom of each other's souls; without the constraints of Thrushcross Grange, he would not have been thrown into hostile violence. It is not, after all, Heathcliff who is so monstrous, but the worlds about him that are so confining. If Society cannot assimilate a natural force, does this not merely prove that it is unnatural?

Heathcliff demands full discussion, but in the end one must come back to Catherine Earnshaw, for it is she, by her relationship with Heathcliff, by her change from an Earnshaw into a Linton, and by her resumption of the earlier bond, who embodies in herself the human-social dilemma at the heart of the book.

3. EMMA AND CATHERINE:
TWO VISIONS COMPARED

It is a sign of the difference between the two books that, while in discussing Emma Woodhouse, it was not necessary to give close attention to Knightley, Heathcliff in Emily Brontë's novel had to be assessed at some length, despite Catherine's centrality. This is because we approach Emma through Emma herself: we share in her outlook even when we condemn her mistakes, and sometimes we may share in her mistakes too. We are never completely identified with her, but also we are never fully detached. How much the reader 'likes' the character will presumably depend on his temperament; Jane Austen herself said that no one would like Emma except herself. But 'liking' is scarcely relevant. We are set in close relationship to her – to this nucleus of vital forces – and we know her (in the way that the author intends us to know her) not only better than we commonly know people in real life, but with far more authority, for we have her creator's assurance that her temperament, her endowments, and her motives, are such and no other. So long as the author preserves our faith and keeps our attention, the resulting experience is the nearest we can ever get to living a different life from our own.

Emily Brontë's whole approach to her central characters is quite different. As we have seen, we are not permitted the illusion of invisible closeness to, for example, Catherine Earnshaw, since her character is filtered to us through that of Nelly Dean. This is of course not entirely true, for the author permits herself the licence of making Nelly repeat whole dialogues verbatim, so that when she reports Catherine's words we have the illusion of hearing Catherine's voice, not Nelly's; moreover, she and the other narrators retail incidents so graphically that they become, for pages at a time, virtually identified with the novelist, and we are afforded the normal illusion of being 'there'. Nevertheless, so far as the inner meaning of events is concerned, we are always aware that we are second-hand witnesses, and that the direct witnesses are in a position to record with unusual faithfulness, but not to understand. The effect is twofold. As we watch Catherine pass from the known, or knowable, to the unknown, we feel the perspective of what we regard as the potentiality of feeling greatly enlarged. She passes from being the ragamuffin of the moors with Heathcliff as her crony into imperious but mellowing young ladyhood as wife of Edgar Linton; so far her tale is a familiar one. But when she declares that her and Heathcliff's souls are one, and when she lives and dies in the key of this assertion in all her adult love for Heathcliff, we realise that she has outburst the familiar, has in a way outburst herself, and that it would be vain for us to try to identify ourselves with her condition, as we can even with the rich, fine love of Hareton and Catherine Linton. Alternatively, the effect may be that we become more critical than we usually are of the scope of feeling that the novel normally presents to us: what the 'social ego' feels is what is social, but what of the ranges of reality outside the social?

Jane Austen, on the other hand, takes society and its limitations for granted as her characters' only element: the fish must swim, however shallow and muddy the water. A better analogy for a Jane Austen novel might be that Society is a game, into which characters are born as players. If he plays the game by the rules, the character becomes its slave, though whether he awakens to the fact will depend on his endowments. But to break the rules is to be sent off the field; this might seem romantic but is actually sordid. Fortunately the rules are maintained by the slaves themselves, and they are by definition rather gross in perception; it remains possible, therefore, to play by one's own rules, and to play all the better, so long as one has the intelligence, the humility, and the experience to enable one to discover what they are. The greatest danger is to imagine that one is escaping from the rules by building them into a fantasy, and this is the error that Emma makes until she is shocked into reality.

If we now refer the analogy to *Wuthering Heights*, we find that we are stationed near the touchline of the game; the players are less likely to be sent off because some of them are only just beginning to walk on; and it is still possible to refuse – as Heathcliff refuses – to acknowledge the game from the start. It is important to remember about Heathcliff, however, that he once tried to join in, when (in order to compete with the young Edgar for Catherine) he told Nelly that he had decided 'to be good'; but he was disqualified forthwith. Heathcliff need not have been a Satan.

Chapter 8

The Heroine Victim 2

GWENDOLEN HARLETH OF *DANIEL DERONDA*
ISABEL ARCHER OF *THE PORTRAIT OF A LADY*

I. A STUDY IN FRUSTRATION

Was she beautiful or not beautiful? and what was the secret of form or expression which gave the dynamic quality of her glance? Was the good or the evil genius dominant in those beams? Probably the evil; else why was the effect that of unrest rather than undisturbed charm? Why was the wish to look again felt as coercion and not as a longing in which the whole being consents?

So the novel opens; Deronda is questioning himself as he watches Gwendolen at a gaming table in Baden.

Compare this with the opening description of *Emma*. Emma is 'handsome, clever, rich . . .'. The terms are practical, assured, not contentious; there will be general agreement about whether a girl is handsome, whereas there will be disagreement about whether she is beautiful. Then comes 'seemed to unite some of the blessings of existence': and we know that the 'seemed' is exactly chosen to implant a strictly calculated quantity of doubt in the reader's mind. In a Jane Austen novel it is the judgement that is challenged, the judgement both of the readers and the characters; we may not have all the facts, but we know that we shall receive them in due course; we may make ridiculous mistakes even with the evidence before us, but we know that they will eventually be exposed. The Austen world is indeed not a simple one. Our judgement – and that of the heroine – must be constantly alert, and it must not be a mere abstracting, mathematical faculty inanimate of feeling. It is not a world of definitions; but it is a world where definition is valid, where ascertainment is feasible.

The world which opens with Deronda's ponderings is one in which the judgement is equally challenged, but it can never be sure of vindication, or of rebuttal; for another more radical faculty is being challenged – our apprehension. What kind of being is Gwendolen, upon whom our imaginative reason has been called to exercise itself? 'Beautiful', 'good', 'evil' – we are thrown at once among the large, contentions terms, and at issue with one another at that. But we, or, at present, Deronda, cannot evade them, because her glance is 'dynamic'; his far-flung speculations are forced upon him by the force of the vitality that emanates from her, even as he stands and watches her. In Chapter IV this vitality is expressed more concretely:

Always she was the princess in exile, who in time of famine was to have her breakfast-roll made of the finest-bolted flour from the seven thin ears of wheat, and in a general decampment was to have her silver fork kept out of the baggage. How was this to be accounted for? The answer may seem to lie quite on the surface: – in her beauty, a certain unusualness about her, a decision of will which made itself felt in her graceful movements and clear unhesitating tones, so that if she came into the room on a rainy day when everybody else was flaccid and the use of things in general was not apparent to them, there seemed to be a sudden, sufficient reason for keeping up the forms of life; and even the waiters at hotels showed the more alacrity in doing away with crumbs and creases and dregs with struggling flies in them.

Yet, characteristically, the author goes on to warn the reader against accepting this favourable account too easily: mere egotism, of which Gwendolen has plenty, is a great force for getting one's own way, and as for her 'potent charm', it is ambivalent:

. . . those who feared her were also fond of her; the fear and the fondness being perhaps both heightened by what may be called the iridescence of her character – the play of various, nay, contrary tendencies. . . . We cannot speak a loyal word and be meanly silent, we cannot kill and not kill in the same moment; but a moment is room enough for the loyal and mean desire, for the outlash of a murderous thought and the sharp backward stroke of repentance.

It will be noticed, that while the authoreal voice of Jane Austen is extremely reticent, and that of Emily Brontë totally silent, George Eliot admonishes the reader freely. At her worst she even harasses him, but most of the time, her admonishments are a necessary constituent of her art of character-creation, for it is her purpose to keep his judgement suspended until his apprehension is wide enough and deep enough; until he has brought to bear on the character *all* his experience of human nature. Yet this insistence on the character being seen in the widest possible scope of moral awareness and human sympathy by no means entails that her character dissolves in vagueness or is cancelled by contradictions, for she is also insisting that the reader should concentrate on her his most sensitive responses and careful discriminations; that he should be alive to inflexions of speech and behaviour. This of course implies the realisation of the character in dialogue and incident. The dialogue has a new variety and flexibility of tone. Here is a specimen, early in the book, of cultured 'party' conversation:

'You are fond of books, as well as of music, riding, and archery, I hear,' Mrs Arrowpoint said, going to her for a tête-à-tête in the drawing-room after dinner: 'Catherine will be very glad to have so sympathetic a neighbour.' This little speech might have seemed the most graceful politeness, spoken in a low melodious tone; but with a twang fatally loud, it gave Gwendolen a sense of exercising patronage when she answered gracefully –
'It is I who am fortunate. Miss Arrowpoint will teach me what good music is: I shall be entirely a learner. I hear that she is a thorough musician.'
'Catherine has certainly had every advantage. We have a first-rate musician in the house now – Herr Klesmer; perhaps you know all his compositions. You must allow me to introduce him to you. You sing, I believe. Catherine plays three instruments, but she does not sing. I hope you will let us hear you. I understand you are an accomplished singer.'
'Oh no! – "die Kraft ist schwach, allein die Lust ist gross," as Mephistoles says.'
'Ah, you are a student of Goethe. Young ladies are so advanced now. I suppose you have read everything.'
'No, really. I shall be so glad if you will tell me what to read. I have been looking into all the books in the library at Offendene, but there is nothing readable. The leaves all stick together and smell musty. I wish I could write books to amuse myself, as you can!

How delightful it must be to write books after one's own taste instead of reading other people's! Home-made books must be so nice.'

For an instant Mrs Arrowpoint's glance was a little sharper, but the perilous resemblance to satire in the last sentence took the hue of girlish simplicity when Gwendolen added –

'I would give anything to write a book!'

'And why should you not?' said Mrs Arrowpoint, encouragingly. 'You have but to begin as I did. Pen, ink, and paper are at everybody's command. But I will send you all I have written with pleasure.'

'Thanks. I shall be so glad to read your writings. Being acquainted with authors must give a peculiar understanding of their books: one would be able to tell then which parts were funny and which serious. I am sure I often laugh in the wrong place.' Here Gwendolen herself became aware of danger, and added quickly, 'In Shakespeare, you know, and other great writers that we can never see. But I always want to know more than there is in the books.'

'If you are interested in any of my subjects I can lend you many extra sheets in manuscript,' said Mrs Arrowpoint – while Gwendolen felt herself painfully in the position of the young lady who professed to like potted sprats. 'These things I daresay I shall publish eventually: several of my friends have urged me to do so, and one doesn't like to be obstinate. My Tasso, for example – I could have made it twice the size.'

'I dote on Tasso,' said Gwendolen.

'Well, you shall have all my papers, if you like. So many, you know, have written about Tasso; but they are all wrong. As to the particular nature of his madness, and his feelings for Leonora, and the real cause of his imprisonment, and the character of Leonora, who, in my opinion, was a cold-hearted woman, else she would have married him in spite of her brother – they are all wrong. I differ from everybody.'

'How very interesting!' said Gwendolen. 'I like to differ from everybody; I think it is so stupid to agree. That is the worst of writing your opinions; you make people agree with you.'

This speech renewed a slight suspicion in Mrs Arrowpoint, and again her glance became for a moment examining. But Gwendolen looked very innocent, and continued with a docile air.

'I know nothing of Tasso except the *Gerusalemme Liberata*, which we read and learned by heart at school.'

'Ah, his life is more interesting than his poetry. I have constructed the early part of his life as a sort of romance. When one thinks of his father Bernardo, and so on, there is much that must be true.'

'Imagination is often truer than fact,' said Gwendolen, decisively, though she could no more have explained these glib words than if they had been Coptic or Etruscan. 'I shall be so glad to learn all about Tasso, – and his madness especially. I suppose poets are always a little mad.'

'To be sure – "the poet's eye in a fine frenzy rolling;" and somebody says of Marlowe –

For that fine madness still he did maintain,
Which always should possess the poet's brain.'

'But it was not always found out, was it?' said Gwendolen, innocently. 'I suppose some of them rolled their eyes in private. Mad people are often very cunning.'

The substance of this conversation might have come from Jane Austen: the ostentation of Mrs Arrowpoint, her actual obtuseness to literary value, her sentimental mixing up of literature and life, making the former a substitute for the latter – she is later very angry on grounds of the social inequality of the match when her daughter marries Klesmer, despite her feelings about Leonora not marrying Tasso. But in the treatment of the characters and in the technique of expression there are differences. In Jane Austen's 'serious' characters, dialogue is on the whole meticulously clear-cut, deliberate, precise, in a word – formalised, while the comic characters tend to be given each an individual idiom – the excited, broken sentences of Miss Bates, the leisurely ceremoniousness of Mr Woodhouse, and so forth. But Gwendolen, though she picks her words carefully, speaks at once carelessly and pointedly, graciously and yet flippantly, with an artlessness which is in the main cunningly assumed, but in some degree authentic; the pace of her speech varies and the intonations are audible. And Mrs Arrowpoint, though she is on the whole an object of ridicule, is kept carefully this side of caricature; in her speech she plunges on, with her 'twang fatally loud', but not clumsily – she is a well-bred woman – and not so stupidly as to fail to see that Gwendolen's artlessness has an edge. As regards character-treatment, there is a greater difference from Jane Austen on Gwendolen's part: she is taking risks of causing offence that a Jane Austen heroine would seldom take – Emma's satirical comment to Miss Bates as to her loquacity is an exception, and bitterly she repents it; in general, Austen heroines mock, or weep, inwardly, and keep an outward graciousness for their butts and their foes, like a shield. It is characteristic of Gwendolen that she expects and gives no such quarter; she ventures more because she wants more, but also because she is far from clear about what she has to lose and whether there is anything distinctly to be gained.

As with Emma and Catherine Earnshaw, we are faced with a problem of egotism. Emma's egotism was a protest against the mere social identity, which, at the conscious level of her mind, she herself took for granted as all she needed; Catherine's egotism was an assertion of that level of her personality which only Heathcliff could reach, a protest against that reduction of self to which Edgar could not but subject her. Gwendolen is as closely involved in society as Emma, but much less secure; she has impulses of freedom as wild as Catherine's, but with a gaming table instead of a moorland, and no Heathcliff. She resembles Emma in being out of stature with her family – all mediocrities who indulge her. She is expected to make a brilliant marriage socially; personally, she expects this to involve union with a wealthy or high-born nonentity. She knows her own brilliance and enjoys shining, but her fears cause her to keep men at bay, by which she gains a reputation for capriciousness and coquettishness that do not express her true nature. Moreover, striking and intelligent as she is, her resources for shining are themselves uncertain. Her ironic intelligence, as we have seen, disturbs and baffles county society, and her talents, as she comes to discover – for at first she sets store by them – are less than those of the true artist. She can be summed up only by mutually frustrating opposites: she is indulged but unguided; independent but forestalled; brilliant but immature; dynamic but dissatisfied; she has deep feelings but no suitable objective for them; she is arrogantly assured, yet at a deep level panic-haunted.

This panic-stricken depth in Gwendolen is a reminder of the existence of an obstacle to the art at least of our earlier novelists.

To express the unconscious in a personality is usually to infringe social reality and the conventions which are part of it, so that, unless a novelist (such as Emily Brontë) had an unusual field at command, the unconscious motives and experience can only be brought to bear indirectly, as in the instance of Emma. The dramatic poets had no such problem; Shakespeare, by his employment of metaphor, could explore and convey the hidden selves of Macbeth, Hamlet, or Othello. The great novelists of the Victorian period began to do the same, but guardedly, through the discreet use of symbol, for fear of shocking the conventions of credibility and prudery. Art, as is well known, can often be the more telling for indirectness, and a character such as Gwendolen, who is hiding the deeper sources of her uneasiness from herself, would not be made artistically more realistic by the novelist choosing to make them explicit. Part of Gwendolen's fear is unconsciously sexual, and this is implied, for example, in her cruel treatment of her cousin Rex, whom in general she likes. However, to overstress her sexual fear is to distort her predicament, which is the discordance between the inner and the outer, the personal and the social; how to reconcile independence with fulfilment in another, as her nature fundamentally but all obscurely requires.

George Eliot's problem being how to illuminate the sources of Gwendolen's basic fear without making her behave unrealistically, she solves it by using as a symbol a picture in her mother's house. The picture shows 'an upturned dead face, from which an obscure figure seemed to be fleeing with outstretched arms', and it is kept locked behind a hinged panel because Gwendolen so dislikes it. On one occasion, Gwendolen is performing a tableau of the supposed statue of Queen Hermione, which awakens to music in *The Winter's Tale*:

'Music, awake her, strike!' said Pauline (Mrs Davilow, who by special entreaty had consented to take part in a white burnous and hood).

Herr Klesmer . . . struck a thunderous chord – but in the same instant, and before Hermione had put forth her foot, the movable panel, which was on a line with the piano, flew open on the right opposite the stage and disclosed the picture of the dead face and the fleeing figure, brought out in pale definiteness by the position of the waxlights. Everyone was startled, but all eyes in the act of turning towards the opened panel were recalled by a piercing cry from Gwendolen, who stood without change of attitude, but with a change of expression that was terrifying in its terror. She looked like a statue into which a soul of Fear had entered: her pallid lips were parted, her eyes, usually narrowed under their long lashes, were dilated and fixed. Her mother, less surprised than alarmed, rushed towards her. . . . But the touch of her mother's arm had the effect of an electric charge; Gwendolen fell on her knees and put her hands before her face. She was still trembling, but mute, and it seemed that she had self-consciousness enough to aim at controlling her signs of terror, for she presently allowed herself to be raised from her kneeling posture and led away, while the company were relieving their minds by an explanation.

Hermione, in Shakespeare's play, has long been thought dead by her husband, and the scene in question is a way of restoring her to him, for she has never in fact died. It is in the very act of making her first movement back to life that Gwendolen is struck motionless by the deathly picture, and the terror it causes her greatly exceeds the slight shock that might have been expected. Why she is so terrified is never explicitly explained; in fact it takes the whole novel to provide the explanation. The picture, like a nightmare, seems to image her state, as though her own living were something like a perpetual flight from her own dying, her own life-in-death, or a deathliness within her. She herself heightens life in all her surroundings, and Hermione is a symbol of life restored, of resurrected love; but Gwendolen in her fearful, proud independence is withheld from the role, for she is also denying the most living part of her nature – the power of her love.

The warning is survived, repressed, explained away, but the incident sends a shaft of illumination into the mystery of Gwendolen's marriage. Superficially there might seem to be no mystery about this: Grandcourt is rich, of great family, has great prospects. All this is important to Gwendolen's relations; what is still more important for Gwendolen herself is that he is personally distinguished, and yet so fastidiously indifferent to vulgar pre-occupations that, with all the resources with which he will provide her for brilliance, she does not fear that he will hinder her freedom. She learns that he has a mistress to whom he already has promised marriage, and runs away to Baden, where Deronda first sees her. There, she learns from her mother that their small family fortune has been lost. She returns to England, and Grandcourt tries again; this time, half remorseful about the mistress but half convincing herself that she is acting in the interests of her family, she accepts him. The element of mystery arises from the nature of Grandcourt himself; here is the description of him on their first encounter – we are seeing him partly through Gwendolen's eyes, and partly through George Eliot's:

He was slightly taller than herself, and their eyes seemed on a level; there was not the faintest smile on his face as he looked at her, not a trace of self-consciousness or anxiety in his bearing; when he raised his hat he showed an extensive baldness surrounded with a mere fringe of reddish-blond hair, but he also showed a perfect hand; the line of feature from brow to chin undisguised by beard was decidedly handsome, with only moderate departures from the perpendicular, and the slight whisker too was perpendicular. It was not possible for a human being to be freer from grimace or solicitous wrigglings; also it was perhaps not possible for a breathing man wide awake to look less animated. The correct Englishman, drawing himself up from his bow into rigidity, assenting severely, and seeming to be in a state of internal drill, suggests a suppressed vivacity, and may be suspected of letting himself go with some violence when he is released from parade; but Grandcourt's bearing had no rigidity, it inclined rather to the flaccid. His complexion had a faded fairness resembling that of an actress when bare of the artificial white and red; his long narrow grey eyes expressed nothing but indifference.

Despite the appearance of flaccidity, Grandcourt is formidable, and his formidability is wholly evil. It is based not merely on his great wealth, position and arrogant selfishness; he has in addition a perfect assumption of his own importance, as complete a disregard of anyone else's, and a total lack of conscience. His authentic personal aristocracy is of a kind that constitutes his final outrage to human nature; it consists in refinement of a sort that enables him to behave with charm and delicacy when it suits his purposes (for instance, in his courtship of Gwendolen, especially when he provides for her mother without offending the sensitive family pride), but is also self-justifying in such a way as to obliterate all other standards. Grandcourt is his own standard, and to be subjected to him, as Gwendolen is when she marries him, is to be subjected to a kind of annihilation: 'Grandcourt,' one critic has said, '*is* death.'

How does such a monster come to reign? Because his conception of his own importance is socially endorsed; his deathliness is set upon a pedestal, and the novel shows how. We see him in a number of lights shed by a number of characters. We see him from the point of view of his uncle Sir Hugh Mallinger, who dislikes him but for family reasons has to treat him diplomatically; from that of his embittered but intimidated mistress; from that of his man of affairs, Mr Lush, who tolerates his insulting arrogance for the sake of the luxurious livelihood he contemptuously provides. Most important of all, however, is the view of Gwendolen's uncle the rector, Mr Gascoigne, who has no connection with him except as his niece's suitor:

This match with Grandcourt presented itself to him as a sort of public affair; perhaps there were ways in which it might even strengthen the Establishment. To the Rector whose father (nobody would have suspected it, and no-one was told) had risen to be a provincial corn-dealer, aristocratic heirship resembled regal heirship in excepting its possessor from the ordinary standard of moral judgements, Grandcourt, the almost certain baronet, the probable peer, was to be ranged with public personages, and was a match to be accepted on broad general grounds, national and ecclesiastical. Such public personages, it is true, are often in the nature of giants which an ancient community may have felt pride and safety in possessing, though, regarded privately, these born eminences must often have been inconvenient and even noisome. But of the future husband personally Mr Gascoigne was disposed to think the best. Gossip is a sort of smoke which comes from the dirty tobacco-pipes of those who diffuse it: it proves nothing but the bad taste of the smoker. But if Grandcourt had really made any deeper or more unfortunate experiments in folly than were common in young men of high prospects, he was of an age to have finished with them. All accounts can be suitably wound up when a man has not ruined himself, and the expense may be taken as insurance against future error. This was the view of practical wisdom; with reference to higher views, repentance had a supreme moral and religious value. There was every reason to believe that a woman of well-regulated mind would be happy with Grandcourt.

Once again, one remarks George Eliot's restraint from caricature. It would be easy to make fun of Gascoigne as the worldly clergyman, and good fun *is* made, but equally important is the other fact, that he is according to his lights – which represent, after all, a kind of truth – a good man. He would not, had he known about Grandcourt's mistress and Grandcourt's promise to her, have approved the marriage. But he does not know that inevasible fact, and his spiritual and moral evasiveness, so intrinsic to him that he is totally unconscious of it, plays a great part in the stupefying of Gwendolen into accepting Grandcourt.

She was silent, and the Rector observed that he had produced some strong effect.

'I mean this in kindness, my dear.' His tone had softened.

'I am aware of that, uncle,' said Gwendolen, rising and shaking her head back, as if to rouse herself out of painful passivity. 'I am not foolish. I know that I must marry some time – before it is too late. And I don't see how I could do better than marry Mr Grandcourt. I mean to accept him, if possible.' She felt as if she were reinforcing herself by speaking with this decisiveness to her uncle.

But the Rector was a little startled by so bare a version of his own meaning from those young lips. He wished that in her mind his advice should be taken in an effusion of sentiments proper to a girl, and such as are presupposed in the advice of a clergyman, although he may not consider them always appropriate to be put forward. He wished his niece parks, carriages, a title . . . but he wished her not to be cynical – to be, on the contrary, religiously dutiful, and have warm domestic affections.

His widely representative brand of stupidity – for he is in no ordinary sense a humbug – has enabled him to endorse Grandcourt as an institution rather than as a man, and by a direct inversion of the true values, he has brought himself to estimate Gwendolen's marriage as institutionally, and *therefore* humanly, a right one.

From the cold, refined, cruelty of her deathly marriage she is rescued by Grandcourt's death in a yachting accident – might she have saved him? – and by Deronda. She is guiltless of her husband's death because his past treatment of her paralyses her responses at the decisive second: the image of the dead face and the fleeing figure arises again. Deronda shows her the first glimmerings of life renewal which has always been the true meaning of that repentance which, taking for granted that it is of supreme moral and religious value, Mr Gascoigne none the less does not seem to have conceived as very hard.

2. A STUDY IN FREEDOM

While this exchange of pleasantries took place between the two Ralph Touchett wandered away a little, with his usual slouching gait, his hands in his pockets and his little rowdyish terrier at his heels. His face was turned towards the house, but his eyes were bent musingly on the lawn; so that he had been an object of observation to a person who had just made her appearance in the ample doorway for some moments before he perceived her. His attention was called to her by the conduct of his dog, who had suddenly darted forward with a little volley of shrill barks, in which the note of welcome, however, was more sensible than that of defiance. The person in question was a young lady, who seemed immediately to interpret the greeting of the small beast. He advanced with great rapidity and stood at her feet, looking up and barking hard; whereupon, without hesitation, she stooped and caught him in her hands, holding him face to face while he continued his quick chatter. His master now had had time to follow and to see that Bunchie's new friend was a tall girl in a black dress, who at first sight looked pretty. . . . Meantime the two other gentlemen had also taken note of the new-comer.

'Dear me, who's that strange woman?' Mr Touchett had asked.

'Perhaps it's Mrs Touchett's niece – the independent young lady,' Lord Warburton suggested. 'I think she must be, from the way she handles the dog.'

Thus Isabel Archer makes her first appearance, welcomed by and welcoming a small dog. Like Gwendolen Harleth, she is first seen through the eyes of a man, but whereas Deronda saw Gwendolen distracted in the midst of distraction, Ralph sees

Isabel merely expectant, a figure of promise on a threshold.

F. R. Leavis has remarked that one difference between the two novels is that Gwendolen is seen from within by a woman whereas Isabel is seen from without by a man. It is not that we never look through her eyes; especially in one very fine chapter – Chapter 42 – we look through them at her marriage; but most of the time we are observing, so that it is not for nothing that the novel is called *The* Portrait *of a Lady*. The reader of a novel is, of course, always an observer, but commonly the novelist at least from time to time inveigles him imaginatively into forgetting his detachment, and for the rest of the time he has something like the status of a privileged ghost, able to pass in and out of the characters' minds at will – not merely the author's will, for the reader is to some extent free to suit his taste in the matter. The difference in this novel is that we are invited to pick up clues, and that having done so, we are left to use them as we think best. Again, to a certain extent this is always so; but George Eliot will elucidate the weight and relevance of her clues, Jane Austen eventually conveys to us (through the narrative) whether we have applied hers rightly, and Emily Brontë enables us to estimate the value of hers by relating them to the calibre of the witness who is narrating them. James selects his clues and relates them to his whole with distinct and delicate artistry, but we seldom learn from him whether we lose or misapply them.

The short passage already quoted shows examples. Isabel is alone; that is to say, she has not waited for her aunt to introduce her, and this for a young lady in 1880 is venturesome. She comes through an 'ample doorway', and is standing before a wide summery park; we learn a little later of the narrowness, financial and social, of her recent New England circumstances, and later still we watch how her present amplitude of prospect becomes more than merely visual, until, in the end, she vanishes from the novel through this same doorway but in the opposite direction, all amplitude gone. The little dog barks towards her, but he is friendly, not hostile, and this she interprets; the little dog prefigures the kind of reception she is to get everywhere, and the trustingness with which she meets it as well as her spontaneity and buoyancy. She wears a black dress because she is in mourning – she is an orphan – and this is a mark not only of pathos but also of portent: she is far more vulnerable than she is aware, and though she is to gain so much, by the end of the book she is to lose nearly all. Hints of gaiety, promise, spaciousness, loss, and death, are all notes distinguishing her; the very man who approaches to greet her is the one who is to love her most, to make her fortune unbeknownst to her, to be misunderstood by her and forsaken; and he is already a sick man waiting to die.

Some of these notes can be picked up immediately, such as the behaviour of the little dog; others are only evident retrospectively or at later readings of the book. The first point to psychology; they are details significant for character and behaviour. Those whose significance only appear later are symbolic details, and they indicate the fable of the character; the moral and spiritual truths which the story is to unfold.

The word fable suggests fairy tale, and Isabel is endowed with some of the quality of a fairy tale princess; as she stands before the ample doorway, she resembles Miranda of Shakespeare's *Tempest*, on the point of uttering the words 'O brave new world that hath such people in't!' James in his preface owns to his sense of enchantment by this sort of heroine, and he quotes there a sentence from George Eliot which refers to Gwendolen Harleth: 'In these frail vessels is borne onward through the ages the treasure of human affections.' Appropriately, she is endowed with a career which summarises like a fairy tale. Ralph's enigmatic mother, Isabel's aunt, like a capricious fairy godmother translates her from her impecunious New England surroundings to this country mansion with its atmosphere (especially for her) of enchantment, where she is wooed by Lord Warburton, a princely English nobleman, and by Caspar Goodwood, a prince of American industry. To her cousin, Ralph Touchett, who conceals his love from her because he knows he has not long to live, she is herself a natural princess deprived of her rightful status by poverty; thus he tells his dying father:

'I should like to make her rich.'

'What do you mean by rich?'

'I call people rich when they are able to meet the requirements of their imagination. Isabel has a great deal of imagination.'

Ralph, accordingly, plays the part of a beneficent wizard; old Mr Touchett leaves her a handsome legacy, which would otherwise have gone to his son.

Now the fairy tale darkens: we have had no evil fairy as yet, but the gift of gold is the cue for her to arise. Madame Merle, American expatriate, talented but poor, charms Isabel for her own ends. She has had a child by Gilbert Osmond, yet another expatriate, also poor but with expensive tastes and living in Italy. Though superficially charming, Osmond is cold-bloodedly selfish, and more for the sake of her daughter (who is ostensibly the child of her father's dead wife) than for Osmond whom she no longer loves, Madame Merle conspires to bring him Isabel's money by contriving her marriage to him. Isobel supposes herself to be in love with Osmond's 'mind', lays her money at his feet, and finds herself perpetually imprisoned in the ogre's palace:

It was the house of darkness, the house of dumbness, the house of suffocation. Osmond's beautiful mind gave it neither light nor air; Osmond's beautiful mind indeed seemed to peep down from a small high window and mock at her. Of course it had not been physical suffering; for physical suffering there might have been a remedy. She could come and go; she had her liberty; her husband was perfectly polite. He took himself so seriously; it was something appalling. Under all his culture, his cleverness, his amenity, under his good-nature, his facility, his knowledge of life, his egotism lay like a serpent coiled in a bank of flowers.

The element of fairy tale continues through the daughter Pansy. Osmond has thought it a good investment to bring her up in a convent to have extraordinary perfection of manner and immaculacy of mind; but with this she has an authentic artlessness and spontaneity of feeling, and, though she is dutiful to her father, since he deprives her of her own young prince she has only Isabel to love and to protect her. Isabel's 'princes', each in his characteristic way, try to rescue Isabel from her own predicament, but she refuses them, and returns from Ralph's deathbed to her evil and now utterly hostile husband.

The fairy tale side of Isabel Archer shows her as a mythic figure. She is beautiful, intelligent, open to life; she has the fearlessness (which at the date of the novel was the concomitant of an American girl's unique freedom) together with the high principle associated with a New England upbringing. The fearlessness and the principle are shown in their raw, comic form in her American journalist friend, Henrietta Stackpole; but Isabel is saved from such rawness by her cultivated, sensitive, searching sympathies – what her cousin Ralph means by her imagination, and what for him represents her potentiality. It is these rich qualities, and above all the last, that make her signify fulfilment to her contrasted lovers. To Warburton, the gifted, handsome, radical peer with a bad conscience about his privileges, she represents the partner who will not only ornament his status but will vitalise it by uniting with it a human ardour with its independent spring of inspiration. To Goodwood, she is the human culmination and justification for the toil to which he has inhumanly devoted himself. By marrying either, she could have been richly happy, but with either the happiness would have been different, and this fact makes it clear to her that the acceptance of either must entail some sacrifice of potentiality in herself. It is Ralph, who renounces her, who alone desires to see the fulfilment of Isabel herself, and even he is not ultimately disinterested. As a slowly dying man, he has had to renounce not only his cousin but all life; his longing is to compensate himself by seeing the fulfilment of the girl whom he has come to care for more than all else he has had to sacrifice.

But this ideal creature throws her spiritual resources after her money, entirely wastes herself upon the egoism of the worthless Osmond. It is in seeking the answer to the question why she does this that we reach the crux of her character, that the psychological clues that James provides us must be decisive. We have to shift to Isabel's point of view, and in his preface James describes how this strategy occurred to him as essential for the character of Isabel to embody full importance:

'Place the centre of the subject in the young woman's consciousness,' I said to myself, 'and you get as interesting and as beautiful a difficulty as you could wish. Stick to *that* – for the centre; put the heaviest weight in *that* scale, which will be so largely the scale of her relation to herself. Make her only interested enough, at the same time, in the things that are not herself, and this relation needn't fear to be too limited.'

The easier and less worth-while alternative, he has just pointed out, would have been to centre the subject in the consciousnesses of those about her: 'Make it predominantly a view of *their* relation and the trick is played. . . .' This he rejects. Yet the very postulation of the alternatives seems to indicate James's externality to Isabel. He begins by contemplating a certain character – and the preface states that the inspiration for the tale began in James's conception of Isabel's character rather than in an imagined situation or set of problems – and then asks himself 'What will she do?' And the answer to that comes through the conception of other characters, who take the problem under their management. Thus, the process seems to be that Isabel's character arises in James's mind as a presence, and suggests certain other characters who will arrange her fate for her; he then gets as close to this presence as his authoreal privilege allows, taking the reader with him. We watch as the author watches, but he carefully selects for us the detail that is relevant.

Here, for instance, is part of the description of Madame Merle as Isabel sees her:

When Madame Merle was neither writing, nor painting, nor touching the piano, she was usually employed upon wonderful tasks of rich embroidery, cushions, curtains, decorations for the chimney-piece; an art in which her bold, free invention was as noted as the agility of her needle. She was never idle . . . and with all this she had always the social quality, was never rudely absent yet never too seated. She laid down her pastimes as easily as she took them up; she worked and talked at the same time, and appeared to impute scant worth to anything she did. . . . If for Isabel she had a fault it was that she was not natural; by which the girl meant, not that she was either affected or pretentious, since from these vices no woman could be more exempt, but that her nature had been too much overlaid by custom and her angles too much rubbed away. She had become too flexible, too useful, was too ripe and too final. She was in a word too perfectly the social animal that man and woman are supposed to have been intended to be; and she had rid herself of every remnant of that tonic wildness which we may have assumed to have belonged even to the most amiable persons in the ages before country-house life became the fashion. Isabel found it difficult to think of her in any detachment and privacy, she existed only in her relations, direct or indirect, with her fellow mortals. One might wonder what commerce she could hold with her own spirit. One always ended, however, by feeling that a charming surface doesn't necessarily prove one superficial; this was an illusion which, in one's youth, one had but just escaped being nourished. Madame Merle was not superficial – not she. She was deep, and her nature spoke none the less in her behaviour because it spoke a conventional tongue. 'What's language at all but a convention?' said Isabel, 'she has the good taste not to pretend, like some people I've met, to express herself by original signs.'

Much of the description is in James's terms – 'she had rid herself of every remnant of that tonic wildness' etc. – but the effect that Madame Merle is producing corresponds scrupulously to Isabel's impression of her. This is what one would expect at this stage of the story; the truth about Madame Merle – that she has raised the technique of living at other people's expense into a fine art – has to emerge later, when Isabel finds it out for herself. But James is not only presenting Isabel's judgement of Madame Merle; he is also presenting clues, very distinct ones this time, to a judgement on Isabel herself. The two women are shown to be in complete contrast; 'that tonic wildness' that Madame Merle is so without makes for the distinctiveness of Isabel's own nature; the commerce which Madame Merle cannot be imagined holding with her own spirit is an interchange which arises spontaneously in Isabel; this girl who respects Madame Merle for not pretending 'to express herself by original signs' is the girl who had said to Mrs Touchett, about the house where her father had died, 'Yes; but I don't dislike it for that . . . I like places in which things have happened – even if they're sad things. A great many people have died here; the place has been full of life.' It is Isabel's 'relation to herself' that is being shown: her very sense of potentiality which elsewhere shows almost as arrogance – the arrogance that can refuse in quick succession an American millionaire and an English peer – translates itself now, in the face of Madame Merle's perfection, into a sense of incompleteness. Humility seems now the prerequisite of potentiality, and when she comes into her legacy, Ralph is disconcerted to see how the responsibility engendered by it weighs her down:

'... Take things more easily. Don't ask yourself so much whether this or that is good for you. Don't question your conscience so much – it will get out of tune like a strummed piano. Keep it for great occasions. Don't try so much to form your character – it's like trying to pull open a tight, tender young rose. Live as you like best, and your character will take care of itself. Most things are good for you; the exceptions are very rare, and a comfortable income is not one of them.' Ralph paused, smiling; Isabel had listened quickly. 'You've too much power of thought – above all too much conscience,' Ralph added. 'It's out of all reason, the number of things you think wrong. Put back your watch. Diet your fever. Spread your wings; rise above the ground. It's never wrong to do that.'
She had listened eagerly, as I say; and it was her nature to understand quickly. 'I wonder if you appreciate what you say. If you do, you take a great responsibility.'

Ralph is of course right: trusting to her own love of life, guided by her own lightning intelligence, Isabel could hardly have gone wrong in ways that experience would not have put right. The mistake he has made is in supposing that his money will empower her for her highest potential flight, whereas it merely paralyses her with self-mistrust. Without the legacy, she had only to ask herself 'What is *my* potentiality?' With it, she has to ask 'What is the potentiality of *that*?' What Ralph has forgotten is the force of the New England puritan ethic.

James, like Conrad, introduced a new element into character creation by the exploitation of international experience: an American writing in Europe, he could delimit the horizons of both cultures, and exploit the fatal discrepancies wherever these horizons fail to coincide – discrepancies which result in special misunderstandings and peculiar vulnerabilities and exposures. It is to these that Isabel falls a victim, and which make her in the truly valuable sense a 'mythic' character. What happened to Miranda when she returned to Milan, and was exposed to the machinations of Antonio?

3. GWENDOLEN AND ISABEL:
THE DIFFERENCES OF APPROACH

Following F. R. Leavis, I have spoken of the externality of James's approach to the creation of Isabel, as opposed to the inwardness of George Eliot's vision of Gwendolen, and this in spite of James's expressed decision to 'place the centre of the subject in the young woman's own consciousness'. A concise way of showing this is the uses to which money and conscience are put in relation to both characters. Gwendolen's mother loses her money, and Gwendolen's conscience is stupefied into enabling her to marry Grandcourt. Isabel comes into money, and this arouses her conscience; it is her conscience which stupefies her into marrying Osmond. Thus both girls marry, in part, for money: Gwendolen to get it, and Isabel to give it; and both thereby immure their souls – 'You were ground in the very mill of the conventional' is Ralph's dying comment on Isabel's fate. But money is only the most external of their pretexts, and in Gwendolen's case it is more inextricably involved with her whole predicament than it is in Isabel's. For Isabel, the acquisition of her money is a kind of miracle, an intervention in her life by fate such as baffles her to account for until she learns that Ralph contrived it out of love; it is like an extraneous force imposing a bias on her life and deflecting its course. Not only does it constitute an anxious preoccupation, but it increases her vulnerability, for her openness inclining to naïvety, her self-criticism amounting to self-depreciation, her inexperience of Europe blinding her to the extent to which civilised externals (in Osmond and Madame Merle) can hide perfidy, her idealism which turns the very opposition from her most devoted friends to Osmond's account, are all only dangerous to her when she has become labelled by her money as eligible. We understand, by the time she is married, very well how the spell upon her has operated, but we also see that it is circumstances that have made the casting of it possible.

Whereas her mother's financial loss is subsidiary to Gwendolen's fate; it is decisive only in a way that something, sooner or later, must have been. She might have escaped Grandcourt, for she had decided against him on learning of his mistress; but by the time she has met Grandcourt, we already know that a drama is being fought out in Gwendolen's soul – a drama with social as well as personal forces and aspects, and destined to have a social stage for its crisis.

No doubt, then, Gwendolen is a richer creation than Isabel, who none the less is a brilliant one. These two are perhaps the most moving of a line, the 'young girls affronting their destinies', to adapt James's description of Isabel, that extends throughout the nineteenth century into the twentieth, from the heroines of Jane Austen to those of D. H. Lawrence. Not all major novelists attempted them: Charlotte Brontë, E. M. Forster and George Meredith are the most important that remain unmentioned; nor is such a family resemblance as that between Gwendolen Harleth and Isabel Archer at all common. But the nineteenth century was the most dramatic in all history for women, who became thereby touchstones and foci for taste and judgement in ways that men were not. The nineteenth century, after all, was the heroic age for women.

Chapter 9

Character and Environment

PIP OF *GREAT EXPECTATIONS*

HENCHARD OF *THE MAYOR OF CASTERBRIDGE*

I. CHARACTER THROUGH SENSATION

I give Pirrip as my father's family name, on the authority of his tombstone and my sister – Mrs Joe Gargery, who married the blacksmith. As I never saw my father or my mother, and never saw any likeness of either of them (for their days were long before the days of photographs), my first fancies regarding what they were like, were unreasonably derived from their tombstones. The shape of the letters on my father's, gave me an odd idea that he was a square, stout, dark man, with curly hair. From the characters and turn of the description, '*Also Georgiana Wife of the Above*,' I drew a childish conclusion that my mother was freckled and sickly. To five little stone lozenges, each about a foot and a half long, which were arranged in a neat row beside their grave, and were sacred to five little brothers of mine – who gave up trying to get a living exceedingly early in that universal struggle – I am indebted for a belief I religiously entertained that they had all been born on their backs with their hands in their trouser-pockets, and had never taken them out in this state of existence.

EVERY great novelist has a distinctive method of portraying character, but the effect which is common to most of them is one of rationalised sensation. That is to say, certain physical features are described or implied, and the character is given characteristic speech, but he is realised principally by indirect means: he interacts with other characters, who respond to him, in situations to which he responds, and his character is the impression thereby produced. Direct sense impressions of a character always, of course, play a part, but the part is commonly subsidiary. It is the distinctiveness of Dickens that his writing conveys direct sensation of character beyond that of almost any other novelist. It is especially the child's vision – direct, concentrated, all the senses alert, and distinguished

156

from the rationalising, more adult vision by presenting the human being in the first place as an object. This is a presentation which does not reduce the liveliness of the character, for to children all objects have a degree of animatedness. Consequently, the Dickens vision also lends itself readily to the vivid presentation, through sensation, of environment, and of human beings in close relationship to it. This gives Dickens an important advantage over most of his predecessors, for in actual life environment does not lie back for human beings to walk in front of it, like actors before sets on a stage; on the contrary it is so involved in them that we cannot dissociate live people from their surroundings. Our total impression of a friend is compounded with all the physical circumstances in which we have known him.

The infant Pip shows how little, for infants, objects are distinguished from the people associated with them by building up images of his parents and brothers from their tomb-stones. The images of his parents are plausible; those of his brothers, bizarre. Yet it is a bizarreness of truth: the little boys who never took their hands out of their pockets are the infants who died too soon ever to know life as active engagement.

So Pip has a sensation of his family, at once completely detached and very intimate, comically alive although conveyed from their tombs. He proceeds to have a sensation of himself, and simultaneously moves on to the next stage; to that of awareness of his surroundings as something distinct and alien:

Ours was the marsh country, down by the river, within, as the river wound, twenty miles from the sea. My first most vivid and broad impression of the identity of things, seems to have been gained on a memorable raw afternoon towards evening. At such a time I found out for certain, that this bleak place overgrown with nettles was the churchyard; and that Philip Pirrip, late of this parish, and also Georgiana wife of the above, were dead and buried; and that the dark flat wilderness beyond the churchyard, intersected with dykes and mounds and gates, with scattered cattle feeding on it, was the marshes; and that the low leaden line beyond was the river; and that the distant savage lair from which the wind was rushing, was the sea; and that the small bundle of shivers growing afraid of it all and beginning to cry, was Pip.

This consciousness of surroundings as distinct from self is the awakening out of infancy into childhood. It is then that life begins to be dramatic, that the question of destiny forms itself: what will my surroundings do to me, and how far can I change them? Even so Pip's drama begins at this point, with the figure of the escaped convict starting up among the graves.

The novel is about growing up. It begins with Pip crossing a threshold, and he is to continue to cross thresholds until the end. We are not immersed in an inward psychological drama; we have no passages such as the flood of self-insight that Emma experiences when she awakens to her love for Knightley, nor the surge of passion into consciousness when Catherine explains to Nelly the difference between her loves for Edgar and for Heathcliff, nor the sombre lucidity with which Isabel describes to herself her marriage, nor the demonstration of Gwendolen moving trancelike into her marriage with Grandcourt. Such things are not in Dickens' genius. There is psychological drama none the less, but it is all thrown outward on to people, places, atmospheres, events, and the story that enmeshes these into a pattern. Yet it is not ultimately the story that endows the novel with such power, but the fable of which the story is the mechanism. The story is about Pip growing up; the fable is about Pip crossing thresholds.

'The dark flat wilderness' of the marshes, on to which convicts escape from their prison ship and where they are recaptured, confines the young Pip to a world of oppression and vulgar-genteel poverty, dominated by his harsh half-sister and his pompous Uncle Pumblechook, and humanised only by his sister's husband, the sweet-souled childlike blacksmith, Joe Gargery. Joe in his decency, innocence, and dignity of feeling is humanly all a contrast to the rest of Pip's environment, but he is illiterate, and to the growing boy he comes to seem another element of this hemming-in, for which the dreariness of the marshes is a symbol and from which, no more than from the prison ship, is there escape.

But he crosses another threshold into another world – that of Satis House, where the deranged Miss Havisham stopped the clock and her life on the morning her bridegroom forsook her, and lives with her adopted niece Estella. Pip gains entry, nominally to entertain Miss Havisham, but really as a practice victim for Estella whom Miss Havisham is training to wreak revenge on men for her own betrayal by one. Suffocatingly confining though it is, compared to the different sort of confinement of the forge Satis House is to the young Pip a kind of enchanted castle, and one whose threshold his tyrants may not cross:

'This,' said Mr Pumblechook, 'is Pip.'

'This is Pip, is it?' returned the young lady, who was very pretty and seemed very proud; 'come in, Pip.'

Mr Pumblechook was coming in also, when she stopped him with the gate.

'Oh!' she said. 'Do you wish to see Miss Havisham?'

'If Miss Havisham wished to see me,' returned Mr Pumblechook discomfited.

'Ah!' said the girl; 'but you see she don't.'

She said it so finally, and in such an indiscussible way, that Mr Pumblechook, though in a condition of ruffled dignity could not protest.

The now barely adolescent Pip, is, as Miss Havisham intends, duly stricken by Estella; he begins to educate and 'improve' himself so as to be the less scorned by her. When he gets a fortune out of the blue, he assumes that it comes from Miss Havisham, who is careful not to deny it, and supposes that she intends him to be Estella's husband. So Pip crosses his third threshold – outwards, this time, away from the marshland. Perversely, however, the forge and the marshland have changed character. Pip's half-sister has been assaulted by a mysterious assailant; the assault has struck her dumb and shattered her wits, but greatly sweetened her temper. Her place in the household economy is taken by a young girl, Biddy, who has helped Pip to educate himself and who loves him. Joe's innocence, Biddy's naturalness, even Mrs Gargery's idiotic benignancy, now give this narrow world an almost paradisal quality. Satis House and his 'great expectations' are combining to make him selfish and self-important, but Pip, though glad to go, is partly aware that he is not only escaping from his world of childhood constraint and suffering, but also forsaking the world of his innocence:

> When I got into my little room, I sat down and took a long look at it, as a mean little room that I should soon be parted from and raised above, for ever. It was furnished with fresh young remembrances too, and even at the same moment I fell into the same confused division of mind between it and the better rooms to which I was going, as I had been in so often between the forge and Miss Havisham's, and Biddy and Estella.

Away from the world of Biddy and Joe Gargery, then, and into that of Jaggers, the grim lawyer who is to administer his fortune till he comes of age, and his poker-faced clerk, Wemmick. From confinement to confinement: Pip now crosses the threshold of Barnard's Inn, where he is to share chambers:

> I thought it had the most dismal trees in it, and the most dismal sparrows, and the most dismal cats, and the most dismal houses . . . that I had ever seen. I thought the windows of the sets of chambers into which those houses were divided were in every stage of dilapidated blind and curtain, crippled flowerpot, cracked glass, dusty decay, and miserable makeshift. . . . A frouzy mourning of soot attired this forlorn creation of Barnard, and it had strewed ashes on its head, and was undergoing penance and humiliation as a mere dust-hole. Thus far my sense of sight; while dry rot and wet rot and all the silent rots that rot in neglected roof and cellar – rot of rat and mouse and bug and coaching stables near at hand besides – addressed themselves faintly to my sense of smell, and moaned, 'Try Barnard's Mixture.'

Yet this is the great world, not yet of wealth, but the antechamber to his expectations. In it he continues to deteriorate, growing more genteel but also more selfish, no nearer Estella who still tantalizes him and farther away from contentment in general. From it, Joe is excluded, as he finds when he makes a visit; not indeed with the abruptness with which Estella excludes Pumblechook from Satis House, but with equal finality by his own innate sensitiveness:

> Pip, dear old chap, life is made of ever so many partings welded together, as I may say, and one man's a blacksmith, and one's a whitesmith, and one's a goldsmith, and one's a coppersmith.

Diwisions among such must come, and must be met as they come.
... You and me is not two figures to be together in London; nor yet
anywheres else but what is private, and beknown, and understood
among friends. It ain't that I am proud, but that I want to be
right, as you shall never see me no more in these clothes.

Joe shows true inner dignity; Pip only has a sense of the
importance of appearances, of the ostensible evidence of gentri-
hood. He is if not quite a hollow sham, on the way to becoming
one, when the truth about the basis not only of his vanity but of
Estella's pride is shockingly revealed to him. She, it turns out,
is the daughter of a murderess and that same convict, Abel
Magwitch, whom Pip as a little boy on the marshes had long
ago helped to escape. Recaptured, Magwitch was deported to
Australia and there made the fortune with which he has endowed Pip, partly from gratitude, but mainly from the desire to
'make' a gentleman – to enjoy vicariously a state of existence
which he was debarred, by no means merely by his crimes, from
ever himself enjoying. It is like a queer parody of Ralph
Touchett's attempt to endow Isabel Archer's spiritual adventure; but Magwitch is not the man even to see the failure of the
experiment, let alone to understand it.

'Yes, Pip, dear boy, I've made a gentleman on you! It's me wot
has done it! ... Look'ee here!' he went on, taking my watch out of
my pocket, and turning towards him a ring on my finger, while I
recoiled from his touch as if he had been a snake, 'a gold'un and a
beauty: that's a gentleman's, I hope! Look at your linen; fine and
beautiful! Look at your clothes better ain't to be got! And your
books too,' turning his eyes round the room, 'mounting up on their
shelves, by hundreds! ... You shall read 'em to me, dear boy! And
if they're in foreign languages wot I don't understand, I shall be
just as proud as if I did.'

Magwitch dies soon after his illegal return, and Pip forfeits
his fortune, which he would any way have renounced, to the
state. He tries to return to the forge, the marshes, and his
innocence; but Biddy has married Joe – it is Pip's turn to be
locked out, this time from the paradise which he had not
appreciated when it was his. Nor does he win Estella (though
Dickens rewrote the end so as to suggest that perhaps, after all,

he did), but he becomes reconciled with Joe, with whom in fact he never actually quarrelled, and then he takes flight abroad as the colleague of a friend, in consequence of the only really good action he performed in the days of his wealth. He leaves the book a new kind of man, convincingly transformed, and yet perceptibly a continuum of the small child of the first page.

But it is the way in which he has been transformed, not the actual transformation, the fable of the man, not the man himself, that constitutes for us the main interest of the character. Dickens does not build up characters of rich, varied inner life. Yet of all English novelists he is perhaps the most famous for his characters – and rightly; and the central character is often valuable to us merely (or, in the case of Pip, mainly, for he is more interesting than most) as a kind of window through which to experience the rest. They are made vivid to us through simplification, but it is not the simplification of caricature, but of unusual intensity; the intensity, as I have put it, of the child's vision. The child does not see all, but the freshness of his perception and the sharpness of his curiosity enables him to see with extraordinary purity and wholeness of response, and whether it is beautiful, grotesque, amusing, or terrifying, he is equally fascinated by it. In *Dombey and Son*, little Paul Dombey spends long spells staring at an ogreish old woman called Mrs Pipchin, and it is with this kind of absorption that Dickens enables us to perceive Mrs Pipchin ourselves.

These Dickens characters are, moreover, doubly reinforced. They are reinforced not only by the environments which they express; but by one another, rather like musical themes in a symphony or an opera. Biddy, for example, in her simplicity and wholesome feeling, is slight if charming by herself, but she gains force of significance by counter-balancing the hard, cold, bitter and brilliant Estella. Estella, on the other hand, acquires pathos by her close association with Miss Havisham, who, having decided that her time has stopped for ever, is also determined that Estella's shall never begin. Miss Havisham's mode of existence is a deathly form of 'contracting out' of life and its problems, a diseased escapism; but Jaggers' clerk, Wemmick, leads a double life and makes up for his professional dourness by contracting out into his own form of escapism, into his ludicrous but carefree cottage castle at Walworth where he keeps his stone-deaf but extremely contented old grandfather. Wemmick's hardness of surface emphasises the hardness-to-the-core of his master, Jaggers, as Wemmick's home intensifies the sombreness of Jaggers' own residence, kept by the single, ex-criminal servant. The heartless parasitic relatives, who hang, unrequited, upon Miss Havisham, are offset by her other relatives, the single-minded, impecunious Pockets, who ignore her; and Pip's sacrifice of personal relations for personal display, is caricatured by Mrs Pocket's neglect of her family for the sake of brooding on her aristocratic origin. Dominating all these contrasts, we have the polar opposition of Magwitch, with his perverted, brutally ignorant ideas of a gentleman, over against the humble, clear-sighted, humane understanding of social differences on the part of Joe Gargery. And from Joe we might begin again, for we have the contrast between Joe's primal sterling wisdom, and the omniscience of what is not worth knowing (except financially) about human frailty, on the part of Jaggers. In short, what readers sometimes mistake at a distance for exaggerated, over-simplified opposition between black and white, becomes, the closer one looks, a varied and intricate pattern of degrees of light and dark, sombreness and absurdity, the characters enhancing one another from various directions until they accumulate into an elaborate composition.

2. ENVIRONMENT AND IDENTITY

One evening of late summer, before the nineteenth century had reached one-third of its span, a young man and woman, the latter carrying a child, were approaching the large village of Weydon-Priors, in Upper Wessex, on foot. They were plainly but not ill clad, though the thick hoar of dust which had accumulated on their shoes and garments from an obviously long journey lent a disadvantageous shabbiness to their appearance just now.

The man was of fine figure, swarthy, and stern in aspect; and he showed in profile a facial angle so slightly inclined as to be almost perpendicular. He wore a short jacket of brown corduroy, newer than the remainder of his suit, which was a fustian waistcoat with white horn buttons, breeches of the same, tanned leggings, and a straw hat overlaid with black glazed canvas. At his back he carried by a looped strap a rush basket, from which protruded at one end the crutch of a hay-knife, a wimble for hay-bonds being also visible in the aperture. His measured, springless walk was the walk of the skilled countryman as distinct from the desultory shamble of the general labourer; while in the turn and plant of each foot there was, further, a dogged and cynical indifference personal to himself, showing its presence even in the regularly interchanging fustian folds, now in the left leg, now in the right, as he paced along.

A 'skilled countryman' steps out of the landscape; he is a-piece with it in his clothes, his implements, his gait, but the 'dogged and cynical indifference' is 'personal to himself'. He is of 'fine figure' and 'swarthy, and stern in aspect' – fairly general attributes, but his profile, 'so slightly inclined as to be almost perpendicular' is again idiosyncratic. Typical, yet highly distinctive, epitomising the rural south-west, but with a powerful individuality: such are the characteristics of Michael Henchard, who is to sell his wife, rise to be Mayor of Caster-bridge, re-marry his wife, and fall into ruin. The cycle of his career will resemble cycles of his native landscape, following a sequence as pre-ordained by his temperament as the seasons are by the climate, but acting under impulses with unpredict-able consequences to himself and others, as the weather afflicts the countryside. The weather being under the rule of the seasons, it is seldom altogether calamitous; an alien intrusion, on the other hand, may destroy or entirely change a rural economy. Thus even the sale of his wife in a fit of drunken resentment – an incident, Hardy tells us in his preface, based on fact – proves reparable. What turns out to be irreparable is a benevolent action: Henchard's impulsive befriending of Donald Farfrae, the emigrant Scotsman on his way to the colonies, and the consequent introduction into his own and Casterbridge life of a different kind of psychological entity. The relationship between them is the axis of the book: they begin as friends, they become antagonists, and in their rivalry Henchard is foredoomed to defeat, not because Farfrae is malignant – he does not even desire to compete – but because he has inherent advantages. Henchard walks out as he walks in, down on his luck, but this time he can never climb back: 'She watched his form diminish across the moor, the yellow rush-basket at his back moving up and down with each tread, and the creases behind his knees coming and going alternately till she could no longer see him.'

The difference between the two men is not one of ability but of adaptability; Farfrae is free of environment. This is not to say that he is indifferent to his native background; he sings Scots songs in the bar of a Casterbridge inn, and thereby draws the admiration of the natives by the sweetness of his nostalgia:

'Danged if our country down here is worth singing about like that!' continued the glazier, as the Scotchman again melodized with a dying fall, ' "My ain countree!" When you take away from among us the fools and the rogues, and the lammingers, and the wanton hussies, and the slatterns, and such like, there's cust few left to ornament a song with in Casterbridge, or the country round.'

But the glazier's envy and disdain arises because he is talking of a real countryside, where he lives, whereas Farfrae is only singing of a sentiment. His background – his very name is a clue – is no longer life to him, but a pretext for an occasional indulgence, a kind of emotional weekend. He also is to become Mayor of Casterbridge, but he never becomes integrated with the town, as Henchard is, except in the sense that he would 'belong' anywhere. Does this make him superior as a human being? He is certainly superior as an economic man; he is also agreeable, humane, sociably civilised, in ways that Henchard is not. Yet it is Henchard who is the centre of the book; who is humanly impressive in a different scale from Farfrae.

Facing the window, in the chair of dignity, sat a man about forty years of age; of heavy frame, large features, and commanding voice; his general build being rather coarse than compact. He had a rich complexion which verged on swarthiness, a flashing black eye, and dark, bushy brows and hair. When he indulged in an occasional loud laugh at some remark among the guests, his large mouth parted so far back as to show to the rays of the chandelier a full score or more of the two-and-thirty sound white teeth that he obviously still could boast of.

That laugh was not encouraging to strangers; and hence it may have been well that it was rarely heard. Many theories might have been built upon it. It fell in well with a temperament which would have no pity for weakness, but would be ready to yield ungrudging admiration to greatness and strength. Its producer's personal goodness, if he had any, would be of a very fitful cast – an occasional almost oppressive generosity rather than a mild constant kindness.

Susan Henchard's husband – in law at least – sat before them, matured in shape, stiffened in line, exaggerated in traits; disciplined, thought-marked – in a word, older.

The qualities suggested in the second of these paragraphs of description are borne out by Henchard's behaviour and speech. Clearly, he has grown – it is some eighteen years since our introduction to him on the first page – into a man of force. There are gaps, but no ghosts, in such a nature, and whenever he acts it is to bring the whole of himself to bear on the object, whether he is inspired by affection, resentment, or remorse. This implies that his will is as strong as his feelings, and hence arises the paradox that he can sustain a resolve over a long period of time, and yet show violent inconsistencies of feeling within a very short period. Thus his bitter self-reproach over the sale of his wife has caused him to renounce strong drink for twenty years; the abstention is an act of will that retains the force of feeling that engendered it. On the other hand, his exaggerated gratitude and devotion to Farfrae for the latter's expert advice in a technical crisis changes within a year or two to resolute hostility, not because Farfrae behaves in any way but irreproachably, but because he returns Henchard's devotion with cooler friendship, dares to oppose him in his motions of extravagance, and is the more successful of the two when he acts independently. So, too, his devotion to Elizabeth-Jane becomes all at once an unreasoning antipathy when he discovers that she is not, after all, his daughter, and then reverts to the extent of concealing her existence from her true father. This action, indeed, is astonishing to himself:

Henchard heard the retreating footsteps of Newson upon the sanded floor, the mechanical lifting of the latch, the slow opening and closing of the door that was natural to a baulked or dejected man; but he did not turn his head. Newson's shadow passed the window. He was gone.

Then Henchard, scarcely believing the evidence of his senses, rose from his seat amazed at what he had done. It had been the impulse of a moment. The regard he had lately acquired for Elizabeth, the new-sprung hope of his loneliness that she would be to him a daughter of whom he could feel as proud as of the actual daughter she still believed herself to be, had been stimulated by the unexpected coming of Newson to a greedy exclusiveness in relation to her; so that the sudden prospect of her loss had caused him to speak mad lies like a child, in pure mockery of consequences.

It is not the first time that Henchard has astonished himself by an action taken on impulse, nor the first impulse to precipitate ruin in a predicament it sought to save. Prudence is the principal gap in his nature; his actions respond instantaneously to his feelings, leaving no interval for calculation or self-inquiry. Loneliness is the key to all his predicaments, not because he is of different make-up from his neighbours, but because he is typical on a larger scale: his friendship oppresses them, and his antagonism alienates, for tact is another of his gaps. He describes a visit to Jersey on business:

'Well, one Autumn when stopping there I fell quite ill, and in my illness I sank into one of those gloomy fits I sometimes suffer from, on account o' the loneliness of my domestic life, when the world seems to have the blackness of hell, and like Job, I could curse the day that gave me birth.'
'Ah now, I never feel like it,' said Farfrae.

Farfrae never suffers from loneliness not because he has any better domestic life – he has, at first, none – but because he brings to bear on every situation and relationship just what and how much in his personality is required, without overwhelming either, as Henchard does with the whole force of his emotions –
'. . . it was quite true . . . that the curious double strands in Farfrae's life – the commercial and the romantic – were very

distinct at times. Like the colours in a variegated cord those contrasts could be seen intertwisted, yet not mingling.'

Without ever consciously attempting to do so, Farfrae subjects Henchard in both fields. Commercially, he begins as Henchard's employee when Henchard is Mayor; he ends as Mayor employing Henchard, and in a very subordinate capacity. Romantically, he marries Lucetta Templeman, who comes to Casterbridge with the express intention of marrying Henchard on the death of his first wife. Commercially, the achievement is due to Farfrae's superior practicality and expert knowledge, together with the violence of his rival's hostility which plays into his hands. But in personal relations, Henchard is entangled in a web of complications, unseen or discerned too late, only partly the consequence of his own rashness although multiplied by his own reactions to them. It is as though (and here we touch on Hardy's best known characteristic as a novelist – his 'philosophy') he is the victim of a monstrous intrigue; and yet no one intrigues against him. His stepdaughter, when, unable to endure his revulsion against her any longer, she goes to live as Lucetta's companion, notices a mask over Lucetta's gate:

> Originally the mask had exhibited a comic leer, as could still be discerned; but generations of Casterbridge boys had thrown stones at the mask, aiming at its open mouth; the blows thereon had chipped off the lips and jaws as if they had been eaten away by disease.... The position of the queer old door and the odd presence of the leering mask suggested one thing above all others as appertaining to the mansion's past history – intrigue.

If the mask is a symbol, it is at the expense of Lucetta as well as Henchard, for Lucetta is destined to die in consequence of a horrible joke of which Henchard is the unwitting cause. He also is its victim, however, for not only does it finally alienate Farfrae, but by removing Farfrae's wife it lays open the way from the Scotsman to Henchard's stepdaughter, so that at the end of the book he loses her doubly – to her real father, and to his enemy.

Yet this intrigue by the fates is not an arbitrary imposition on the story by the novelist. There is no intrigue against Farfrae; he prospers, and it is as accordant with his nature to do so as it is accordant with Henchard's to suffer. As Farfrae is free of environment, so, by virtue of the same qualities, he is free of victimisation by environment; his nature that is to say is comparatively immune from that larger nature of which Henchard's human nature is essentially a part. There is continuity, in this rural, pre-industrial environment, between countryside and town, and between town and man. Casterbridge is thus described:

> Thus Casterbridge was in most respects but the pole, focus, or nerve-knot of the surrounding country life; differing from the many manufacturing towns which are as foreign bodies set down, like boulders on a plain, in a green world with which they have nothing in common. Casterbridge lived by agriculture at one remove further from the fountain-head than the adjoining villages – no more.

As Casterbridge is to the country round, so Henchard is to the people of the town – their 'pole, focus, or nerve-knot', whereas Farfrae is as a foreign body set down. As he is slighter physically than Henchard, so he is slighter humanly. He is now the man of business, now the lover, now the town official, his nature specialising itself out to the need of the moment; Henchard, in every capacity, is always and wholly Henchard, unable so to specialise himself, but for that reason unable to reduce his own stature. But nature is notoriously indifferent to the fate of its individuals; so Henchard is a victim of his own outstanding individuality. Left to itself, it is not in the nature of human life to be felicitous, and Hardy emphasises this by the use of another symbol – that of the circular earthworks of the great Roman amphitheatre, called the Ring, outside the town, much used for secret interviews and the scene of Henchard's own most fateful encounters:

> Why, seeing that it was pre-eminently an airy, accessible, and sequestered spot for interviews, the cheerfullest form of those occurrences never took kindly to the soil of the ruin, would be a curious inquiry. Perhaps it was because its associations had about

them something sinister. Its history proved that. Apart from the sanguinary nature of the games originally played therein, such incidents attached to its past as these: that for scores of years the town gallows had stood at one corner; that in 1705 a woman who had murdered her husband was half-strangled and then burnt there in the presence of ten thousand spectators. Tradition reports that at a certain stage of the burning her heart burst and leapt out of her body, to the terror of them all, and that not one of those ten thousand people ever cared particularly for hot roast after that. In addition to these old tragedies, pugilistic encounters almost to the death had come off down to recent dates in that secluded arena, entirely invisible to the outside world save by climbing to the top of the enclosure. . . .

It is on the site of such heinous 'entertainment' that Henchard meets his first wife to arrange their re-marriage, and Lucetta, who should have been his second wife, to arrange the return of her love letters. The letters go astray, and it is by a primitive, cruel entertainment in keeping with those associated with the Ring – a kind of public exposure by pageant – that Lucetta's death is brought about.

Hardy quotes Novalis regarding Henchard – ' "Character is Fate", said Novalis, and Farfrae's character was just the reverse of Henchard's, who might not inaptly be described as Faust has been described – as a vehement gloomy being who had quitted the ways of vulgar men without light to guide him on a better way.' But Henchard is no mere blunderer; he is a representative character with a representative fate. We are groping towards Everyman again, but it is an Everyman of a pre-industrial past, of the disappearance of which Hardy spent his own lifetime in contemplation. Despite his constant blunders, Henchard maintains dignity, and it increases at the end, when he returns for one sight of his stepdaughter before her marriage to Farfrae. Gentle as she is, she is now alienated from him, and, in half understanding of the facts, reproaches him for his concealment of her from her father:

Henchard's lips half parted to begin an explanation. But he shut them up like a vice, and uttered not a sound. How should he, there and then, set before her with any effect the palliatives of his great

CHARACTER AND ENVIRONMENT

faults – that he had himself been deceived in her identity at first. . . ; that, in the second accusation, his lie had been the last desperate throw of the gamester who loved her affection better than his own honour? Among the many hindrances to such a pleading was this, that he did not sufficiently value himself to lessen his sufferings by strenuous appeal or elaborate argument.

Waiving, therefore, his privilege of self-defence, he regarded only her discomposure. 'Don't ye distress yourself on my account,' he said, with proud superiority. 'I would not wish it – at such a time, too, as this I have done wrong in coming to 'ee – I see my error. But it is only for once, so forgive it. I'll never trouble 'ee again, Elizabeth-Jane – no, not to my dying day! Good-night. Good-bye!'

A point easy to overlook in an account such as I have given is that Henchard, with all his turbulent impulsiveness, is repeatedly capable of restraint – not of his feelings, but of his behaviour. In most of the occasions when he is 'in the dock' he shows such restraint; it derives from a pride that underlies his arrogance and is closely related to a deep spiritual humility. It is not a denial of feeling, but the manifestation of his feeling at its deepest.

Such restraint on Henchard's part causes him to win the reader's sympathy at times when his conduct might naturally alienate it. So, when his relations with Farfrae begin to cool –

On this account Henchard's manner towards Farfrae insensibly became more reserved. He was courteous – too courteous – and Farfrae was quite surprised at the good breeding which now for the first time showed itself among the qualities of a man he had hitherto thought undisciplined, if warm and sincere. The corn-factor seldom or never put his arm upon the young man's shoulder so as to nearly weigh him down with the pressure of mechanised friendship.

That 'mechanised' is queer, for, on first consideration, Henchard seems the antithesis of mechanisation. (It is for instance Farfrae who introduces farm machinery into the neighbourhood, and Henchard who predicts its futility.) But a man whose behaviour is out of scale with his relationships may be described either as an incalculable force of nature or as a machine out of control, and both descriptions fit Henchard. His periodic dignity in restraint – other examples are his exposure by the disreputable old furmity woman whom he is in the act of trying as a magistrate, and the scene where he is declared a bankrupt – is the redress to the balance.

Moreover, there is a social explanation for the extravagance of his nature. Throughout the book, though this is never stressed, the rural economy of England is slowly declining, and at the beginning of it Henchard's resentment against his colourless wife is that premature marriage has ruined his chances of prospering when times are already hard. He is a representative figure partly because his whole life is a protest against the forces that invisibly work his ruin, much as the forces of industrialisation work the general ruin of the peasantry from beyond the rural horizon. Farfrae understands these changes, and can make use of them; he is the modern, urban, economic man as Henchard is the traditional rural one. With the best will towards Henchard, he cannot help driving him out of Casterbridge, although it is to Henchard's early assistance that he owes all his success. Even so, the industrial England could not help driving the men off the land and thus destroying the older England from which it had itself arisen.

3. CHARACTER THROUGH ENVIRONMENT

Other novelists besides Dickens and Hardy used environment to convey texture of character in the nineteenth century: Scott, the Brontës, and George Eliot are the most distinguished examples. In Scott and the Brontës, however, there were special regional explanations for this use; and in George Eliot it was a by-product of her way of seeing individuals as entities within larger entities – village, town, or class. Hardy was also a regional novelist, but he was one by choice and not merely by personal origin: his interest in people is continuous with his interest in place; to some extent, the people *are* the place, or if they are not, that is one of the most important things about them. Dickens, like George Eliot, saw his individuals in terms of larger entities, but he did not always, scientifically speaking, understand these. (George Eliot can be recommended as social

history; Dickens, only with reserve.) He did, however, understand the environment of such entities – what it meant to live
in and be a part of it. His London is a physical presence, with
real streets, whereas one knows even less of the streets of George
Eliot's Middlemarch than one does about Jane Austen's Highbury, or her Bath; and this has very little to do with whether the
place is itself a fiction. Thus, for different reasons, the sense of
place in association with people is commonly more deliberate
and more intense in Dickens and Hardy than it is in other
nineteenth-century novelists.

This does not mean that these two were greater; it is not
necessarily a virtue to see character in terms of place, and one
does not miss the physical presence of it in *Middlemarch* and
Emma, where, indeed, it may be said to be present by implication. None the less, this 'spirit of place', when it is presented
with the force for conviction that Dickens and Hardy command,
is a great enhancement of vividness and truth in character, and
there are reasons for this enhancement in addition to those
already given.

One enhancement is relevant to Dickens. The animatedness
of his inanimate scenes is imparted to the most inconsiderable
characters, and thence to the more important ones, until the
central character is thrown into relief against the rich lifelike-
ness of his surroundings, thus acquiring interest from them even
though he may lack it intrinsically. An adequate example is
the boy Pip's impression of Pumblechook's shop:

It appeared to me that he must be a very happy man indeed, to
have so many little drawers in his shop; and I wondered when I
peeped into one or two of the lower tiers, and saw tied-up brown
paper packets inside, whether the flower-seeds and bulbs ever
wanted of a fine day to break out of those jails, and bloom.
It was in the early morning after my arrival that I entertained
this speculation. . . . In the same early morning, I discovered a
singular affinity between seeds and corduroys. Mr Pumblechook
wore corduroys, and so did his shopman; and somehow, there was a
general air and flavour about the corduroys, so much in the nature
of seeds, and a general air and flavour about the seeds, so much in
the nature of corduroys, that I hardly knew which was which. The

same opportunity served me for noticing that Mr Pumblechook appeared to conduct his business by looking across the street at the saddler, who appeared to transact *his* business by keeping his eye on the coachmaker, who appeared to get on in life by putting his hands in his pockets and contemplating the baker, who in his turn folded his arms and stared at the grocer, who stood at his door and yawned at the chemist. The watchmaker, always poring over a little desk with a magnifying glass at his eye, and always inspected by a group in smock-frocks poring over him through the glass of his shop-window, seemed to be about the only person in the High-street, whose trade engaged his attention.

From the drawers to the seeds, the seeds to corduroys, the corduroys to Mr Pumblechook, and from Pumblechook all down the street from one to the next stationary shopman, and we end by having not only the setting (so bare that at first it might seem that nothing could be said about it) but the child who makes it all out, and the light, fanciful, yet faintly sardonic humour of the description endows Pip with the suggestions of vitality and the street with its suggestions of stagnancy – a contrast which at this stage of the story is important for Dickens' purposes.

The other enhancement that I propose to mention is relevant to Hardy. Hardy, unlike Dickens, does not animate his in-animate surroundings but he follows a reverse process – that of subduing his background characters into their environment so that this has a human as much as a material texture. The principal characters stand out but with the same consistency – unless like Lucetta Templeman and Donald Farfrae they are 'foreigners', and then it is their very 'alienness' that is their dominant characteristic; and since it is a negative one, they are commonly somewhat colourless or unconvincing. (Donald Farfrae is an exception, because he *has* a background, although it is one he has forsaken.)

The effect of this subduance of the minor characters is not to make them merely lay-figures – the environment is felt too keenly for that – but to give them a kind of generalised force which recalls the characterisation of the Middle Ages and of the Renaissance. Solomon Longways, Christopher Coney, Mother

Cuxsom, and the rest, have their due individuality, but it is individuality which exists to reinforce their communal distinctiveness, and this throws up into relief the sombreness – made of the same stuff as he is – of Henchard's loneliness. It also endows them with force of choral function. The following dialogue occurs outside the church while Henchard and his wife are re-marrying; so far as their observers know it is their first marriage:

'As for thee, Christopher, we know what ye be, and the less said the better. And as for he – well, there – (lowering her voice) 'tis said 'a was a poor parish 'prentice, that began life wi' no more belonging to 'en than a carrion crow.'

'And now he's worth ever so much a minute,' murmured Longways. 'When a man is said to be worth ever so much a minute, he's a man to be considered!'

Turning he saw a circular disc reticulated with creases, and recognised the smiling countenance of the fat woman who had asked for another song at the Three Mariners. 'Well, Mother Cuxsom,' he said, 'how's this? Here's Mrs Newson, a mere skellinton, has got another husband to keep her, while a woman of your tonnage have not.'

'I have not. Nor another to beat me. . . . Ah, yes, Cuxsom's gone, and so shall leather breeches!'

'Yes; with the blessing of God leather breeches shall go.'

' 'Tisn't worth my old while to think of another husband,' continued Mrs Cuxsom. 'And yet I'll lay my life I'm as respectable born as she.'

'True; your mother was a very good woman – I can mind her. She were rewarded by the Agricultural Society for having begot the greatest number of healthy children without parish assistance, and other virtuous marvels.'

' 'Twas that that kept us so low upon the ground – that great hungry family.'

'Ay. Where the pigs be many the wash runs thin.'

'And dostn't mind how mother would sing, Christopher?' continued Mrs Cuxsom, kindling at the retrospection; 'and how we went with her to the party at Mellstock, do ye mind? – at old Dame Ledlow's, farmer Shinar's aunt, do ye mind? – she we used to call Toad-skin, because her face were so yaller and freckled, do ye mind?'

'I do, hee-hee, I do!' said Christopher Coney.

'And well do I – for I was getting up husband-high at that time – one-half girl, and t'other half woman, as one may say. And canst mind' – she prodded Solomon's shoulder with her finger-tip, while her eyes twinkled between the crevices of their lids – 'canst mind the sherry-wine, and the zilver snuffers, and how Joan Dummett was took bad when we were coming home, and Jack Griggs was forced to carry her through the mud; and how 'a let her fall in Dairyman Sweetapple's cow-barton, and we had to clane her gown wi' grass – never such a mess as 'a were in?'

'Ay – that I do – hee-hee, such doggery as there was in them ancient days, to be sure! Ah, the miles I used to walk then; and now I can hardly step over a furrow!'

Their reminiscences were cut short by the appearance of the re-united pair – Henchard looking round upon the idlers with that ambiguous stare of his, which at one moment seemed to mean satisfaction, and at another fiery disdain.

Such dialogue establishes livingly the communal roots of Henchard, as well as showing his present status relative to them. And the following, Shakespearian in its cadence – one thinks of Mistress Quickly on the death of Falstaff – endows the very nonentity of Mrs Henchard with its distinct melody:

'And she was as white as marble-stone,' said Mrs Cuxsom. 'And likewise such a thoughtful woman, too – ah, poor soul – that a' minded every little thing that wanted tending. "Yes," says she, "when I'm gone, and my last breath's blowed, look in the top drawer o' the chest in the back room by the window, and you'll find all my coffin clothes; a piece of flannel – that's to put under me, and the little piece is to put under my head; and my new stockings for my feet – they are folded alongside, and all my other things. And there's four ounce pennies, the heaviest I could find, a-tied up in bits of linen, for weights – two for my right eye and two for my left," she said. "And when you've used 'em, and my eyes don't open no more, bury the pennies, good souls, and don't ye go spending 'em, for I shouldn't like it. And open the windows as soon as I am carried out, and make it as cheerful as you can for Elizabeth-Jane." '

Chapter 10

Human Subject and Human Substance

STEPHEN DEDALUS OF *A PORTRAIT OF THE ARTIST*
RUPERT BIRKIN OF *WOMEN IN LOVE*

I. THE CLIMAX OF INDIVIDUATION

Once upon a time and a very good time it was there was a moocow coming down along the road and this moocow that was coming down along the road met a nicens little boy named baby tuckoo. . . .

His father told him that story: his father looked at him through a glass: he had a hairy face.

He was a baby tuckoo. The moocow came down the road where Betty Byrne lived: she sold lemon platt.

> O, the wild rose blossoms
> On the little green place.

He sang that song. That was his song.

> O, the green wothe botheth.

When you wet the bed first it is warm then it gets cold. His mother put on the oilsheet. That had the queer smell.

His mother had a nicer smell than his father. She played on the piano the sailor's hornpipe for him to dance. He danced:

> Tralala lala,
> Tralala tralaladdy,
> Tralala lala,
> Tralala lala.

Uncle Charles and Dante clapped. They were older than his father and mother but uncle Charles was older than Dante.

Dante had two brushes in her press. The brush with the maroon velvet back was for Michael Davitt and the brush with the green velvet back was for Parnell. Dante gave him a cachou every time he brought her a piece of tissue paper.

The Vances lived in number seven. They had a different father and mother. They were Eileen's father and mother. When they were grown up he was going to marry Eileen. He hid under the table. His mother said:

– O, Stephen will apologise.

Dante said:

– O, if not, the eagles will come and pull out his eyes. –
Pull out his eyes,
Apologise,
Apologise,
Pull out his eyes.

Apologise,
Pull out his eyes,
Pull out his eyes,
Apologise.

As in the beginning of *Great Expectations*, we are immersed at once into an infant world. But the twentieth century has opened, and this is a different kind of vision; one might put it that this writer has eaten of the fruit of science. Whereas by a flash of imaginative insight Dickens concentrates infant sensations, Joyce coolly maps them. Another and allied difference of technique is that whereas the infant Pip is introduced by the voice and through the mind of the adult Pip, re-living his past, the infant Stephen comes to us with his own voice, through his own mind; we are, so to speak, situated within his skull, and we learn his environment as he learns it, with his sharp but at first sight disconnected impressions.

The structure of the passage is really very deliberate and purposive, for this is not any infant, nor even merely a representative Irish infant of the later nineteenth century; it is Stephen Dedalus, whose fate it will be to undergo alienation from Ireland and its Church, but who none the less is to discover a mode of experience that validates his loneliness, and enables him to achieve identity. We start the book at the point at which he is defining himself over against his surroundings, and so the father is mentioned first, and there is more about him than there is about the mother, for he feels over against his father (who 'looked at him through a glass') while his feelings towards his mother (who 'had a nicer smell') are of more comfortable union.

The novel is to describe the growing antagonism of Stephen on the one side and Irish politics and Irish religion – themselves grown reciprocally antagonistic – on the other; his father is to be identified with the politics, and his mother with the religion. The more difficult break – the real one, for it will be enacted in the depths of his personality – is to be with his mother. The last lines of the book are quoted from Stephen's diary:

April 26. Mother is putting my new secondhand clothes in order. She prays now, she says, that I may learn in my own life and away from home and friends what the heart is and what it feels. Amen. So be it. Welcome, O life! I go to encounter for the millionth time the reality of experience and to forge in the smithy of my soul the uncreated conscience of my race.

April 27. Old father, old artificer, stand me now and ever in good stead.

The mother, though forsaken, is still there – in *Ulysses* her spectre is to make him a terrible visitation – but the father has been replaced by Stephen's namesake, the demigod – Dedalus, the skilled artificer. In the initial passage, religion has not begun and the mother is secure. But there is already faint revulsion to the father, and politics make their mysterious entry in the shape of hair-brushes. And then there is the song – 'his song' – the dance, and the verbal jingle, implying the fascination for 'the artificer' of words, music, rhythm; finally, the bashfulness that causes him to hide under the table foreshadowing the great issue of sex.

Thus the reader is launched into the character of Stephen Dedalus as into a current of prose which gathers force as he grows up. We are not always afloat – we are sometimes moving along the bank and watching him with comparative objectivity; but on the whole, we learn him as we learn ourselves, and other characters loom up at us as they do in real life, vivid but partial. The very completeness with which we know the one character entails a sacrifice of that fictional omniscience by which, in the 'traditional' mode of character creation, a novelist shows a reader all round a number of characters. In *Great Expectations* Joe Gargery or Mr Pumblechook does not unfold and become more complex as the young Pip grows up: they are at the end of the book what they were at the beginning. In *A Portrait* we see the characters always from Stephen's angle of vision, and our impressions are dependent on what, at a given stage of growth, he is capable of assimilating. Thus the great quarrel scene over the Christmas dinner table between Dante and Mr Casey – Church versus Parnell – has Dickensian objectivity and vividness, but its power arises from our experiencing it through the boy's consciousness. The scene begins cosily:

All were waiting: uncle Charles, who sat far away in the shadow of the window, Dante and Mr Casey, who sat in the easy chairs at either side of the hearth, Stephen, seated on a chair between them, his feet resting on the toasted boss. Mr Dedalus looked at himself in the pier-glass above the mantelpiece, waxed out his moustache ends and then, parting his coat tails, stood with his back to the glowing fire; and still from time to time he withdrew a hand from his coat tail to wax out one of his moustache ends. Mr Casey leaned his head to one side and, smiling, tapped the gland of his neck with his fingers. And Stephen smiled too for he knew now that it was not true that Mr Casey had a purse of silver in his throat. He smiled to think how the silvery noise which Mr Casey used to make had deceived him. And when he had tried to open Mr Casey's hand to see if the purse of silver was hidden there he had seen that the fingers could not be straightened out: and Mr Casey had told him that he had got those three cramped fingers making a birthday present for Queen Victoria.

Mr Casey tapped the gland of his neck and smiled at Stephen with sleepy eyes: and Mr Dedalus said to him:

– Yes. Well now, that's all right. O, we had a good walk, hadn't we, John? Yes . . . I wonder if there's any likelihood of dinner this evening. Yes . . . O, well now, we got a good breath of ozone round the Head today. Ay, bedad.

He turned to Dante and said:

– You didn't stir out at all, Mrs Riordan?

Dante frowned and said shortly:

– No.

Nothing could be more reposeful, apart from the faint sign of Dante's ill humour, but before the meal is half over it ends in violence, grotesque comedy, tragic pathos:

– No God for Ireland! he cried. We have had too much God in Ireland. Away with God!

– Blasphemer! Devil! screamed Dante, starting to her feet and almost spitting in his face.

Uncle Charles and Mr Dedalus pulled Mr Casey back into his chair again, talking to him from both sides reasonably. He stared before him out of his dark flaming eyes, repeating:

– Away with God, I say!

Dante shoved her chair violently aside and left the table, upsetting her napkinring which rolled slowly along the carpet and came to rest against the foot of an easychair. Mr Dedalus rose quickly and followed her towards the door. At the door Dante turned round violently and shouted down the room, her cheeks flushed and quivering with rage:

– Devil out of hell! We won! We crushed him to death! Fiend!

The door slammed behind her.

Mr Casey, freeing his arms from his holders, suddenly bowed his head on his hands with a sob of pain.

– Poor Parnell! he cried loudly. My dead king!

He sobbed loudly and bitterly.

Stephen, raising his terrorstricken face, saw that his father's eyes were full of tears.

The episode is important not only for the disputed issues, which are to become for Stephen his Scylla and Charybdis, but for its claustrophobic intensity and coarseness which come to oppress him even worse. Environment, once more, has an intimate relationship to character, and as in *Great Expectations* it manifests itself by its pressure of confinement. The nature of this confinement superficially varies from the lower middle-class Dedalus household to the Jesuit school and college, but a common oppressiveness underlies them: a curious compound of moral effect on the growing Stephen is of all-round repulsion; his nature is fastidious and liberal, and he finds himself chilled, degraded, repressed.

– And thanks be to God, Johnny, said Mr Dedalus, that we lived so long and did so little harm.

– But did so much good, Simon, said the little old man gravely. Thanks be to God we lived so long and did so much good.

Stephen watched the three glasses being raised from the counter as his father and his two cronies drank to the memory of their past. An abyss of fortune or of temperament sundered him from them. His mind seemed older than theirs: it shone coldly on their strifes and happiness and regrets like a moon upon a younger earth. No life or youth stirred in him as it stirred in them. He had known neither the pleasure of companionship with others nor the vigour of rude male health nor filial piety. Nothing stirred within his soul but a cold and cruel and loveless lust. His childhood was dead or lost and with it his soul capable of simple joys and he was drifting amid life like the barren shell of the moon.

> Art thou pale for weariness
> Of climbing heaven and gazing on the earth,
> Wandering companionless. . . ?

He repeated to himself the lines of Shelley's fragment. Its alternation of sad human ineffectiveness with vast inhuman cycles of activity chilled him and he forgot his own human and ineffectual grieving.

This aesthetic abstraction into which he is caught while groping among his personal distresses is typical, and the only genuine liberation from the flux of encounters available to him. But genuine as it is, by its nature it is temporary only, and affords him no help in the self-disgust of his daily living in an alien environment. Segregated by his fastidiousness, his strong sensual impulses drive him to whoring, but, unlike his contemporaries, in no spirit of mere escapade. His spirit is too serious for that, and since only the Church takes his adventures as seriously as he does, he is swept by a sermon into an appalled sense of sin:

Time was to sin and enjoy, time was to scoff at God and at the warnings of His holy church, time was to defy His majesty, to disobey His commands, to hoodwink one's fellow men, to commit sin after sin and to hide one's corruption from the sight of men. But that time was over. Now it was God's turn: and He was not to be hoodwinked or deceived. Every sin would then come forth from its lurking place, the most rebellious against the divine will and the most degrading to our poor corrupt nature, the tiniest imperfection and the most heinous atrocity.

So the priest; one remarks the sonorous melody of his periods. The Church captivates Stephen by its aestheticism – it is difficult to imagine him being so impressed by a plainer, more 'Protestant' appeal – and at the same time demands his submission with its eloquent menaces. His self-disgust is precipitated into self-loathing and terror. He confesses, and is blessedly released; he enters into a phase of intense piety. In the end, however, the effect is entirely negative. He is relieved of his self-abhorrence, but the ties, previously severed, with his world are not renewed; his revolted fastidiousness is not reconciled and his seething energies remain unfulfilled.

The crisis that now arises seems to issue from the assertiveness of his sensibility. He has a hypnogogic faculty for transmitting his experience into visual terms and this bars his submission to the Church in its disembodied nature:

> The Reverend Stephen Dedalus, S.J.
> His name in that new life leaped into characters before his eyes and to it there followed a mental sensation of an undefined face or colour of a face. The colour faded and became strong like a changing glow of pallid brick red. Was it the raw reddish glow he had so often seen on wintry mornings on the shaven gills of the priests? The face was eyeless and sour-favoured and devout, shot with pink tinges of suffocated anger. Was it not a mental spectre of the face of one of the jesuits whom some of the boys called Lantern Jaws and others Foxy Campbell?

The Church, for Stephen, repeatedly dissolves back into men, as the peremptoriness of his senses magnetizes him from abnegation back into selfhood. His decision to enter the university, thereby estranging his parents, is more than a mere renunciation of vocation for priesthood; it is acknowledgement of a different call, the mere contemplation of which is a liberation of his spirit.

Two issues arising from the character of Stephen Dedalus remain to be discussed. The first: what is the real nature of this enlargement and fulfilment that he seeks? For we solve little by merely denominating it 'the life of art'. The second: what sort of creative motivation lies behind the character; put in another way, what kind of reality does the product represent?

In a dialogue near the end of the book, Stephen's friend

Cranly forces him to declare himself: 'I will not serve that in which I no longer believe, whether it call itself my home, my fatherland, or my church: and I will try to express myself in some mode of life or art as freely as I can and as wholly as I can, using for my defence the only arms I allow myself to use – silence, exile, and cunning.'

Again we have a 'contracting out' of the environment, as in *Great Expectations*, but here as a very explicit and conscious choice. Stephen's disbelief is inspired by the emotions rather than the intellect, but the intellect plays its part for the themes of religion and country enter into the very home. Yet earlier in the conversation Stephen has declared that he neither believes nor disbelieves in the eucharist, and Cranly has remarked that despite Stephen's lack of belief his mind is still supersaturated with religion. There is much talk of the mother in connection with religion, and of Stephen's lack of love: '– I tried to love God, he said at length. It seems now I failed. It is very difficult. I tried to unite my will with the will of God instant by instant. In that I did not always fail. I could perhaps do that still. . . .' What sort of disbelief is this? One infers that it is the manifestations of household, nation, and church that Stephen is rejecting, rather than the essences of human relationship, country and religion. These essences, or others which take their place, are to be rediscovered in Stephen's own self; and before we protest against his selfish arrogance, we should remember that the teaching of twentieth-century psychology has been that the individual has access through his preconscious to sources of vitality which the conscious, social ego may repress and deny, so that the self in its loneliness may, given adequate courage, insight, and honesty, have resources which are denied to society in its debased, fragmented, and incomplete responsiveness to human needs. Art, we infer, is to be Stephen's medium, for this alone has responded with positive life at these depths; but the choice is none the less one that involves the most terrible risks:

– You made me confess the fears that I have. But I will tell you also what I do not fear. I do not fear to be alone or to be spurned for another or to leave whatever I have to leave. And I am not afraid to make a mistake, even a great mistake, a lifelong mistake, and perhaps as long as eternity too.

Cranly, now grave again, slowed his pace and said:

– Alone, quite alone. You have no fear of that. And you know what that word means? Not only to be separate from all others but to have not even one friend.

– I will take the risk, said Stephen.

– And not to have any one person, Cranly said, who would be more than a friend, more even than the noblest and truest friend a man ever had.

His words seemed to have struck some deep chord in his own nature. Had he spoken of himself, of himself as he was or wished to be? Stephen watched his face for some moments in silence. A cold sadness was there. He had spoken of himself, of his own loneliness which he feared.

– Of whom are you speaking? Stephen asked at length.

Cranly did not answer.

So the loneliness that is to Stephen opportunity, the condition of life, is to Cranly deprivation, and Stephen, in his diary, concludes that it is maternal deprivation that Cranly is brooding on: the science of psychology is once again flashing its beam.

But it is not an intermittent beam; it is a steady enfolding one that dictates the organisation of the book. Instead of a continuous narrative, incident linked to incident so as to afford an illusion of consecutive development as happens when one reconstructs on logical principles the development of one's own past, the episodes are superficially fragmented, the only consecutiveness being chronological, rather as though one were to make jottings about one's past as they happened to occur to one. Yet that 'happened to occur', of course, conceals a hidden dictate; the mind recalls what it is offered from a hidden source, not on logical but on psychological principles of relevance, the degree of the relevance being apparent from the intensity of the recall. The episodes of greatest intensity will resemble watersheds in a landscape, determining its structure. There are three such watersheds in *A Portrait*: the Christmas dinner scene; the sermon episode; and the epiphany scene near the end, when Stephen watches the girl bathing her feet in the stream. The first and the second stand out each with its own sufficiency; they might be stories from Joyce's sequence, *The Dubliners*, but this effect of standing in relief enhances their structural force. The first is traumatic: the child's quiet ecstasy in domestic union is crushed by the violent impingement of the public, external disputes so that the security of his innocence is permanently disrupted, and at the same time he is transfixed into permanent alienation from both sides. This is like a thesis dividing into antitheses. In the second the antitheses, in the shape of carnality and spirituality, eros and caritas, the two kinds of love, fight their battle in his own soul. In the outcome, the divine love gains a complete, but illusory, victory; the basic alienation has been overlaid but not dissolved. It is the 'epiphany' scene, erotic yet contemplative, ecstatic yet tranquil, its high tension at the same time a spiritual balance, which expresses the true synthesis, the authentic enlargement of the spirit into the outer world: ' "Heavenly God!" cried Stephen's soul, in an outburst of profane joy.' The word 'profane', originally, meant 'outside the temple'; Stephen's spirituality has hitherto been locked inside himself in antagonism to the outer world, as the Irish Church has been in acknowledged antagonism to Irish patriotism, and the mother in unacknowledged antagonism to the father; now it floods forth, rushes to its freedom.

Such then is Stephen's case-history, and we find that it has a dialectical pattern. But the book is, after all, a work of art, and this means that, clinically speaking, it is not a case history at all. On the other hand, behind Stephen Dedalus stands James Joyce; the novel is to some extent an autobiography. As such it presents, for us, for the first time in an acute form, specific problems: the relationship of the author to the character who is his image, and how far we can or ought to distinguish between them. If the identity is complete, the book will not be a novel but mere autobiography, which *A Portrait* is assuredly not; in so far as it is incomplete, as the hero is a free creation, it will not be an authentic but only an imaginative case-history. It is safer to regard *A Portrait* as more novel than case history, but the large autobiographical element has the function of a control, enabling the reader to suspend his disbelief, for which earlier writers relied on a large measure of social or metaphysical acceptance.

2. THE RECOVERY OF COMMUNITY

Ursula and Gudrun Brangwen sat one morning in the window-bay of their father's house in Beldover, working and talking. Ursula was stitching a piece of brightly-coloured embroidery, and Gudrun was drawing upon a board which she held on her knee. They were mostly silent, talking as their thoughts strayed through their minds.

'Ursula,' said Gudrun, 'Don't you *really want* to get married?' Ursula laid her embroidery in her lap and looked up. Her face was calm and considerate.

'I don't know,' she replied. 'It depends how you mean.'

Gudrun was slightly taken aback. She watched her sister for some moments.

'Well,' she said, ironically, 'it usually means one thing! But don't you think anyhow, you'd be – ' she darkened slightly – 'in a better position than you are in now?'

A shadow came over Ursula's face.

'I might,' she said. 'But I'm not sure.'

Again Gudrun paused, slightly irritated. She wanted to be quite definite.

'You don't think one needs the *experience* of having been married?' she asked.

'Do you think it need *be* an experience?' replied Ursula.

'Bound to be, in some way or other,' said Gudrun, coolly. 'Possibly undesirable, but bound to be an experience of some sort.'

'Not really,' said Ursula. 'More likely to be the end of experience.'

Gudrun sat very still, to attend to this.

'Of course,' she said, 'there's *that* to consider.' This brought the conversation to a close. Gudrun, almost angrily, took up her rubber and began to rub out part of her drawing. Ursula stitched absorbedly.

'You wouldn't consider a good offer?' asked Gudrun.

'I think I've rejected several,' said Ursula.

'*Really!*' Gudrun flushed dark – 'But anything really worth while? Have you *really*?'

'A thousand a year, and an awfully nice man. I liked him awfully,' said Ursula.

'Really! But weren't you fearfully tempted?'

'In the abstract, but not in the concrete,' said Ursula. 'When it

187

CHARACTER IN ENGLISH LITERATURE

comes to the point, one isn't even tempted – oh, if I were tempted, I'd marry like a shot. I'm only tempted *not* to.' The faces of both sisters lit up with amusement.

'Isn't it an amazing thing,' cried Gudrun, 'how strong the temptation is, not to!' They both laughed, looking at each other. In their hearts they were frightened.

How far we have got from 'a large measure of social or metaphysical acceptance' can be seen from this dialogue. It is not that the formal attitudes are so changed from those of previous heroines over the century before. Emma Woodhouse was 'tempted not to marry', because she believed herself emotionally as self-sufficient as she was financially. Catherine Earnshaw was 'tempted not to marry' Edgar Linton for reasons not very different from Ursula's, though but for Heathcliff the point of view would not have occurred to her. Isabel Archer refuses two very eligible men because she will not deprive herself of her future, although she is poor; Gwendolen marries because without marriage she cannot imagine any future, but her attitude to men is close to that of Ursula and Gudrun – she even employs the same tone of flippant scorn. Intrinsically, however, the sisters differ from their predecessors in two ways: they contemplate the institution of marriage with a new scepticism, an unprecedented detachment, and yet 'in their hearts they were frightened'. It is the combination which is above all new, for Gwendolen had the fear and the other three, in their different ways, had the emancipation; here we have the emancipation leading to the fear. If it is not only no longer a social inevitability but also become barren as a soil for personal union, then marriage, this most central of all social institutions, has lost its validity, and society is meaningless to its heart.

The book, with this opening dialogue, moves thus swiftly to its central issue: what constitutes the meaningfulness of human relationships, and what frustrates them, makes them a lie. We are not asked to accept the evidence of two young girls on the edge of experience; the issue is raised again and again by a wide range of people in very different situations. We have Mrs Crich at her son's wedding reception: '*I* don't know people whom I find in the house. The children introduce them to me – "Mother this is Mr So-and-so". I am no further. What has Mr So-and-so to do with his own name? – and what have I to do with either him or his name?' We have her husband's unsuccessful attempt to run his mines on the Christian precept – 'Perhaps he had loved his neighbour even better than himself – which is going one better than the commandment.' On the other hand, his son Gerald is only too successful in running them mechanistically:

'Certainly, he's got go,' said Gudrun. 'In fact I've never seen a man that showed signs of so much. The unfortunate thing is, where does his *go* go to, what becomes of it?'
'Oh I know,' said Ursula. 'It goes in applying the latest appliances.'

Hermione Roddice, patroness of intellectuals, wants universal recognition of equality in the spirit, but her emotion is received in silence, and then Rupert Birkin, the school inspector, trounces her: 'It's just the opposite, just the contrary, Hermione. We are all different and unequal in spirit – it is only the *social* differences that are based on accidental material conditions . . .' and the German sculptor, Loerke, considers that the machine is all: '. . . nothing but this, serving a machine, or enjoying the motion of a machine – motion, that is all. You have never worked for hunger, or you would know what god governs us.' Idealism is thus again and again brought up against dependence on machine; the first is in its various forms false, and the second futile. But the ideas are not abstracted from their exponents; indeed it is their function to expound the characters that utter them, rather than the other way round – above all, to expound their relationships. We have, accordingly, no Shavian debates though there are plenty of discussions; but the discussions are instrumental to the characterisation, and the characterisation is worked through multiple relationship – not merely with other characters but with environment and animals, by the technique of symbolism.

In Lawrence, the characters do not explain themselves; they discover themselves. True, every character we have considered has been engaged in self-discovery, but his creator – or so the reader feels – in some sense and degree 'has known' what is to be discovered; the reader commits himself to the writer as to God, secure that, if he does so alertly and not blindly, the character will unfold so that what is hidden in his destiny shall be made manifest. But Lawrence begins further back. His ruthless scepticism takes nothing for granted, so that we are not offered characters who unfold, but characters who are seeking what exists in them to be unfolded; or, to express it in theological terms, they are not trying to save their souls, but to know whether they have souls, and if so, what they are. These are philosophical questions, if philosophers allow them to have any meaning, but in real life they have to be lived, and this novel dramatizes the living of them.

We have had characters starting their careers in given social organisations; we have seen the characters evolving through, in spite of, against, and out of their societies. In *Women in Love* too, the social organisation is weightily established: we have the great houses, Breadalby and Shortlands, the bohemian society of London, and the coal-mines of Chapter 17 – 'The Industrial Magnate'. But the opposition between individual and society is overt from the first page, and what I have called 'contracting out' – seeking fulfilment outside the social forms – is treated realistically, extensively, and radically; it becomes in fact the crucial part of the book. In *Great Expectations* it is little more than escape, of the right sort or the wrong; in *Daniel Deronda*, where it is relevant to Daniel but not to Gwendolen, it is little more than aspiration; in *A Portrait of the Artist* it is the climax, but the book ends on its threshold. In *Women in Love* it carries the four central relationships through to their conclusion: the union in opposition of Ursula and Rupert Birkin, the antagonism of Gudrun and Gerald Crich, the estrangement of the sisters, the failure of the friendship between Rupert and Gerald. The success of the one relationship and the failure of the other three are at the deepest level, beyond all danger in the one, beyond all remedy in the others; a success in relationship and a failure in community.

The novelist, then, takes us far within the personality, into the pre-social, pre-conscious regions, out of which both personality and community must arise, if at all. His problem, evidently, must be how to afford us enlightenment there, since 'light' is ostensibly a factor of the daylight, conscious part of our world. It is not, however, a new problem; we do not need psychologists to tell us of the pre-conscious, for, as a reviewer of one of the earlier books by Freud pointed out, his method of exploring it had long been that of the poets, that is to say, illumination by reflection from symbols. Freud's discovery was that symbols could be used analytically, whereas the poets had used them synthetically, as, for instance, Shakespeare in *Macbeth*; but both methods may be diagnostic, the difference of course being that the poetic diagnosis will itself be symbolic. Thus *Women in Love* and its characters all the time have a dual nature: the characters are presented as actual but their truth is for us symbolic; so in turn they have experiences which for them are actual but whose truth for them as well as for us is symbolic. This, too, is not new; something of the sort might be said of every novel, though of some more easily than of others – for instance of Dickens more easily than of Jane Austen; it is the difference, again, between story and fable. The newness lies in this, that not only the novelist but the characters themselves are critically conscious of this duality in their world. We have met this critical consciousness already in the opening dialogue: 'Marriage, yes, but what after all does marriage mean? Experience or the end of experience?' Behind the question is implied another – 'What *is* experience?' For us, this question projects still another: 'A novel has characters, yes, but what *is* character?'

This critical, challenging spirit in the characters is both heightened and controlled by the fact that the leader of the central nucleus of four, Rupert Birkin, is a projection of Lawrence himself. The difference between this projection and that of Stephen Dedalus from Joyce is that Stephen's career is emancipation from false relationships, whereas Birkin's is the discovery of true ones; and linked with this is the difference that on the one hand Stephen's artistic vocation is all-important, while on the other Birkin has no vocation, his post of school inspector being merely a convenience. He heightens the relationships in the book, because his existence enables Lawrence to propound the issues directly, and he controls the relationships by representing Lawrence's own critical spirit. But he is not above the arena; he does not know all the answers and keep everyone in order. He meets with opposition and failure as well as success, and he is subjected to criticism and ridicule. The temper of the writer will decide whether an auto-biographical element simplifies, sentimentalises, and dissipates the feeling in a book, or whether it does the opposite – exposes more of it, strengthens and enriches it. It is Lawrence's achievement to have accomplished, with some lapses, the second.

Through Birkin we learn what may be called Lawrence's psychology and metaphysic of the human personality. In the first place, it is life that matters to him, not merely his life, or human life.

Birkin looked at the land, at the evening, and was thinking: 'Well, if mankind is destroyed, if our race is destroyed like Sodom, and there is this beautiful evening with the luminous land and trees, I am satisfied. That which informs it all is there, and can never be lost. After all, what is mankind but just one expression of the incomprehensible. And if mankind passes away, it will only mean that this particular expression is completed and done. That which is expressed, and that which is to be expressed, cannot be diminished. There it is, in the shining evening. . . .'

This, however, is not an idea so much as a mood, and must stand in its context. Birkin is in a train, sitting opposite Gerald Crich with whom he has been having a pessimistic discussion.

'. . . I want the finality of love.'
'The finality of love,' repeated Gerald. And he waited for a moment.
'Just one woman?' he added. The evening light, flooding yellow along the fields, lit up Birkin's face with a tense, abstract steadfastness. Gerald still could not make it out.
'Yes, one woman,' said Birkin.
But to Gerald it sounded as if he were insistent rather than confident.
'I don't believe a woman, and nothing but a woman, will ever make my life,' said Gerald.

'Not the centre and core of it – the love between you and a woman?' asked Birkin.

Gerald's eyes narrowed with a queer dangerous smile as he watched the other man.

'I never quite feel it that way,' he said.

'You don't? Then wherein does life centre, for you?'

'I don't know – that's what I want somebody to tell me. As far as I can make out, it doesn't centre at all. It is artificially held *together* by the social mechanism.'

Birkin pondered as if he would crack something.

'I know,' he said, 'it just doesn't centre. The old ideals are dead as nails – nothing there. It seems to me there remains only this perfect union with a woman – sort of ultimate marriage – and there isn't anything else.'

Gerald's scepticism in the face of life goes with an aggressiveness of feeling in connection with love – his 'queer dangerous smile' is a hint of it. It is the feeling, rather than the opinion, that counts. Birkin, equally sceptical in opinion, has a 'tense, abstract steadfastness' in his face, disclosing more convincingly than his 'insistent rather than confident' words his underlying faith. But the difference is not merely the simple oppositions of doubt against faith, or aggressiveness against responsiveness; Birkin retains the capacity to live in the unison of his whole being; just as it is he who responds to the radiance of the landscape, and to relate it to their conversation, so it is he who feels oppressed by the deathliness of London when they enter it. Gerald, who does not respond with any vividness to either, has the deeper layers of his self in suspension; his own centre is in his consciousness. The scene in which he forces his panicking horse to stand at the level-crossing while the goods-trucks clatter by, and the scene in which he forcibly restrains his sister's rabbit, tearing to be free, are images of his own psyche. And both incidents are watched by the appalled Gudrun, whom at the end of the book, before he goes to his own death, he tries to kill.

The contrast between the two men issues more explicitly in the chapter entitled 'Totem' when they are looking at the African carving of a woman in labour.

N   193

'Why is it art?' Gerald asked, shocked, resentful.

'It conveys a complete truth,' said Birkin. 'It contains the whole truth of that state, whatever you feel about it.'

'But you can't call it *high* art,' said Gerald.

'High! There are centuries and hundreds of centuries of develop-ment in a straight line, behind that carving; it is an awful pitch of culture, of a definite sort.'

'What culture?' Gerald asked, in opposition. He hated the sheer barbaric thing.

'Pure culture in sensation, culture in the physical consciousness, really ultimate physical consciousness, mindless, utterly sensual. It is so sensual as to be final, supreme.'

But Gerald resented it. He wanted to keep certain illusions, certain ideas like clothing.

'You like the wrong things, Rupert,' he said, 'things against yourself.'

'Oh, I know, this isn't everything,' Birkin replied, moving away.

Later in the book, when the compound of attraction and antagonism between the two men has become strongly marked, Birkin is to wonder whether Gerald isn't a portent of a con-trasted but analogous development in the white races: 'Was this then all that remained? Was there left now nothing but to break off from the happy creative being, was the time up? Is our day finished? Does there remain to us only the strange, awful after-wards of the knowledge in dissolution, the African knowledge, but different in us, who are blond and blue-eyed from the north?' Birkin is no longer anticipating the death of man with equanimity, and again we have to see his mood in its context. It comes in 'Moony', after Birkin, watched by Ursula unseen in the darkness, tries to smash the image of the moon reflected in a pool. The moon is to him for the moment Cybele, ancient Mother of the Gods and so the prototype of all females, and his actions are a dreamlike expression of his resentment against his dependence on and need for her. When Ursula makes her presence known to him, they have a dialogue, both a quarrel and a love-scene, in which each fights the assertiveness of the other's ego. It is next day that he is struck by the alternative dis-solutions, that of sensual knowledge and of conscious knowledge, the two slaveries, and sees marriage as release from them;

marriage as he means it – 'a . . . free proud singleness, which accepted the obligation of the permanent connection with others, and with the other, submits to the yoke and leash of love, but never forfeits its own proud individual singleness, even while it loves and yields'. Upon which he goes to her home to propose to her, and finds himself embroiled in a triangular clash of wills between himself, Ursula's father, and Ursula herself.

Throughout the book, Birkin is at war with the assertive ego and its instrument the will, whether the will is used for repression and aggression, as in the case of Gerald Crich, or to expound a false synthesis, as in the aspirations of Hermione Roddice. But the assertive will is a human constituent so that he himself possesses one, and finds himself repeatedly under attack from Ursula on just this account. Nor, even when he recognises the justice of her attack, will he merely submit to her, for in her very appeals to his 'love' he sees the half-conscious desire of the female to subject the male, and the temptation to submit is a degradation and dissolution of the self. And yet there is a sense in which the male has to be dominant, and another in which he has to submit. He and Ursula watch the love-play of the two cats, Mino and Minette, in Birkin's garden:

> He, going statelily on his slim legs, walked after her, then suddenly, for pure excess, he gave her a light cuff with his paw on the side of her face. She ran off a few steps, like a blown leaf along the ground, then crouched unobtrusively, in submissive, wild patience. The Mino pretended to take no notice of her. He blinked his eyes superbly at the landscape. In a minute she drew herself together and moved softly, a fleecy brown-grey shadow, a few paces forward. She began to quicken her pace, in a moment she would be gone like a dream, when the young grey lord sprang before her, and gave her a light handsome cuff. She subsided at once, submissively.

As cats, they live their own lives remote from human beings; as male and female animals, they are close; in their exquisite beauty and rightness they have something, if it could be discovered, to teach. Between Birkin and Ursula an argument starts; it begins playfully, but it grows serious, and though the cats are forgotten, they permeate it. She won't allow him to be the dominating tom, and indeed his didacticism cuts an awkward figure after Mino's graceful antics. He, on the other hand, rejects her use of the word 'love', fearing the corrupting influence of its decadent romantic and decadent Christian associations. In the end, however, he is overcome by her subtle, feline charm and has to submit. He has understood the cats' game better than she, but she has learnt to use it.

Through stormy, passionate, intricate scenes, shot with tenderness, Ursula Brangwen and Rupert Birkin learn their way into union with each other. Ursula discovers the answer to the doubt she expressed in the opening conversation with her sister: marriage to Birkin is not the end of experience, but the beginning. It is Gudrun's affair with Gerald which works out according to Ursula's prediction. The fate of the other two relationships in the book – that between the sisters, and the friendship between Gerald and Birkin – are dependent on the love affairs, and the more important and more difficult of the two is the friendship. Gerald is the more distinctively and aggressively masculine, physically the more active, spiritually the more helpless. He needs the subtlety of Birkin's wider consciousness and the boldness of his more adventurous intelligence, while Birkin, on the other hand, through Gerald learns and affirms his own masculinity. In 'Gladiatorial', Birkin visits Gerald after his rebuff by Ursula when he formally proposes to her, and finds him in a state of inanition and thankful for the visit:

Something dead within him just refused to respond to any suggestion. He cast over in his mind, what it would be possible to do, to save himself from this misery of nothingness, relieve the stress of this hollowness. And there were only three things left, that would rouse him, make him live. One was to drink or smoke hashish, the other was to be soothed by Birkin, and the third was women.

They strip, and have a friendly wrestling match to the point of physical exhaustion. This creates a kind of affirmation between them; a masculine bond through the relief to their differently restless and unsatisfied natures, and it is a physical intimacy which men in their usual relationships are debarred from achieving, except, for instance, under the stress of war. It is a bond arising from different spiritual states however, and so an impermanent one; they can only meet in tension. Two images figure the incompleteness, the basic destructiveness, of Gerald's thwarted personality. One arises when he dives again and again into the lake at Shortlands to recover the body of his drowned sister, and it is relevant to the scene that as a boy Gerald had accidentally shot his brother:

'. . . But it's curious how much room there seems, a whole universe under there; and as cold as hell, you're as helpless as if your head was cut off.' He could scarcely speak, he shook so violently. 'There's one thing about our family, you know,' he continued. 'Once anything goes wrong, it can never be put right again – not with us. I've noticed it all my life – you can't put a thing right again – not with us. I've noticed it all my life – you can't put a thing right, once it has gone wrong.'

They were walking across the high-road to the house.

'And do you know, when you are down there, it is so cold, actually, and so endless, so different really from what it is on top, so endless – you wonder how it is so many are alive, why we're up here. . . .'

The depths he has been plunging into are not only those of the lake, as Gerald knows. But the upper mind has its great desolate expanses. Near the end of the book, Gerald organises an Alpine holiday:

The next day, they descended at the tiny railway station of Hohenhausen, at the end of the tiny valley railway. It was snow everywhere, a white, perfect cradle of snow, new and frozen, sweeping up on either side, black crags, and white sweeps of silver towards the blue pale heavens.

As they stepped out on the naked platform, with only snow around and above, Gudrun shrank as if it chilled her heart.

'My God, Jerry,' she said, turning to Gerald with sudden intimacy, 'you've done it now.'

Instinctively she feels that he has taken them to a kind of absolute, from which there will be no descending. It is Gerald's absolute, where he is to die. The book ends with the following conversation between Ursula and Rupert Birkin:

'Did you need Gerald?' she asked one evening.

'Yes,' he said.

'Aren't I enough for you?' she asked.

'No,' he said. 'you are enough for me, as far as a woman is concerned. You are all women to me. But I wanted a man friend as eternal as you and I are eternal.'

'Why aren't I enough?' she said. 'You are enough for me. I don't want anybody else but you. Why isn't it the same with you?'

'Having you, I can live all my life without anybody else, any other sheer intimacy. But to make it complete, really happy, I wanted eternal union with a man too: another kind of love,' he said.

'I don't believe it,' she said. 'It's an obstinacy, a theory, a perversity.'

'Well – ' he said.

'You can't have two kinds of love. Why should you!'

'It seems as if I can't,' he said. 'Yet I wanted it.'

'You can't have it, because it's false, impossible,' she said.

'I don't believe that,' he answered.

It is an awkward, flat, broken dialogue, but it is meant to be, for here are two exhausted people, momentarily out of sympathy on a crucial issue. From it, the mystical word 'eternal' protrudes incongruously, but Birkin (like Christian) was never afraid to appear ridiculous. The relationship itself would have had meaning, but the bright vision of it has gone, leaving only 'eternal union with a man', like a formula for one of the stale ideals that Birkin despised so much. Like the opening one, this closing dialogue ends on a note of doubt; with Birkin and Gerald, there has been an end of experience. Is there another meaning? At the cost of possible simplification, it is tempting to associate the four leading characters with the four Jungian functions in man: Birkin stands for intuition, and Ursula for the physical, inarticulate; Gerald Crich is then the rational, organising function, and Gudrun figures the emotions. In their union, there would be unity, a whole, but the rational and the emotional forces have torn themselves away: it is natural that the intuitive partner should discern the loss, and that the satisfied, physical partner should be baffled at the insight. But if this description looks like an attempt to summarise the book by a diagrammatic formula, it had better be forgotten.

3. THE PROBLEM OF CHARACTER

Writing to Edward Garnett about his previous novel, *The Rainbow*, Lawrence says:

> You mustn't look in my novel for the old stable *ego* of the character. There is another *ego*, according to whose action the individual is unrecognisable, and passes through, as it were, allotropic states which it needs a deeper sense than any we have been used to exercise, to discover are states of the same single radically unchanged element. (Like as diamond and coal are the same pure single element of carbon. The ordinary novel would trace the history of the diamond – but I say, 'Diamond, what! This is carbon.' And my diamond might be coal or soot, and my theme is carbon.)

'Allotropic' means varying in physical properties without changing in substance. In the usual nineteenth-century novel, Lawrence seems to be saying, we meet characters as we meet them in life – in a social relationship; that is to say, in judging them, we bring to bear certain social assumptions implied by the author, so that the characters are psychological entities within a social mould or framework. He means, I think, that we only see such characters on a horizontal plane, on the level at which they have conscious dealings with other men and women: coal and diamonds are acceptable substances with a recognisable 'exchange' value. Yet this stable ego whom we watch and hear talking, who works and loves and kills and dies, has other states of being of which he is unaware or at least inarticulate, and yet which work upon him fully as powerfully as his social pressures. Jane Austen's character is a woman even more than she is Emma Woodhouse, with all the social references which the name, once one has read the novel, calls to mind. We saw how the 'personal' Emma at last breaks through the falsifying mould, but what is this 'personal' Emma? What is the nature of this being, how did it arise, what sustains it? We are not told; the character is a 'datum'. Nor does Jane Austen need to tell us, not so much because the reader is unlikely to ask, as because she is concerned with a different question: since we have personalities and live in society, how do we manage? It is useless to ask questions that are irrelevant to the one that you are trying to answer, and misleading to say, as some modern critics do say, that we have to take sides between the authors who ask different sorts of questions; for instance, between Jane Austen and D. H. Lawrence.

By Lawrence's time, the social references had become confused, contradictory, partly meaningless, no longer cohesive and therefore no longer definitive; the 'stable' ego was no longer stable (even in appearance) in real life, and so he was forced to look deeper, to try to find the carbon behind the coal and the diamond and the soot. *Women in Love*, indeed, shows us these 'egos' clearly enough, but they are broken down, and it is in their breaking down and their attempts to re-form that their interest consists. Nor are the novelists who come between these two content merely to repeat the question which Jane Austen asked; each, according to his or her temperament, his or her social disposition, and the phase of the century, questions different assumptions in a new way. Emily Brontë, writing as she does from a highly independent consciousness and with an unusual social perspective, is almost as radical as Lawrence himself in her own way, and yet George Eliot, with her angle of vision (a more normally advantageous one, but for that very reason less conducive to fundamental reinterpretation), goes as far into the conditions that lie behind conscious behaviour, and is extensively critical of the assumptions that lie behind social pressures such as Jane Austen was obliged to take for granted. But if the questions are different, the concern is the same: the maintenance, discovery, achievement, or creation of integrity in the individual, when all the time forces within and outside are trying to falsify him or tear him apart. Surveying them with this concern in our minds, we may find the novelists less at variance than they seem at first; if Jane Austen's heroines seem to lack normal sensuality, this is not because, as Lawrence thought, she is old maidish, but because it is assumed; it is there in their liveliness, and it is not from there that their problems of integrity arise.

An interesting distinction at every period of the novel is between those characters who end in union or communion with another or others, and those who end alone, and this difference goes back to those fictions which initiate the novel: Christian enters the great community of the saints with Hopeful, but Crusoe ends a solitary. Pip, bereft of his earthly paradise with Joe and Biddy and failing to achieve Stella, ends as an essentially lonely figure; Isabel Archer is decidedly one, and Michael Henchard even more; Stephen's aloneness is even his goal. Emma ends, on the contrary, on the brink of happy marriage, and the ghost of Catherine Earnshaw walks the moors with Heathcliff – in union if only after death – while her daughter is in bliss with Hareton. Gwendolen Harleth ends in loneliness enough, it is true, but this is not conclusive, for she is to seek her way back to human relationship from her penitent bereavement; *Women in Love* ends in both union and loss. The difference cannot easily be explained by saying that one set of writers is basically hopeful about the human lot, while the other is pessimistic, for Dedalus and Crusoe are content with their destinies, and confident, while George Eliot, Emily Brontë and D. H. Lawrence load their conclusions with question marks. But perhaps, at least at the time of writing, there was a genuine difference of emphasis in the interest in character of the two classes of writer, as though the ones who end their characters' careers in aloneness are finally concerned with the character as he is by himself, whereas those who end with union, either predictable or achieved, are more preoccupied with human relationship. No creator of character, of course, can ignore either aspect, but a difference of emphasis may exist, though it may vary from one phase to another of an author's work, as, perhaps, between early and late Dickens.

Whether or not the difference can be held valid for the novelists of the nineteenth century, it is strongly marked in our last two, for Joyce constantly returns to the theme of loneliness, while Lawrence is as positively concerned with the life of relationship. Joyce carries the self-consciously lonely ego to its logical conclusion with Mr Bloom in *Ulysses*, while Lawrence continues to search for the ground of all union. In doing so, Lawrence carries us back to those medieval and renaissance writers for whom Man was more real and more important than men; who saw men as intelligible or otherwise in terms of a more or less felt intelligibility in the universe. Looking back on the people of Chaucer and of Shakespeare, on Sir Gawayn and Everyman, they may seem to us now larger than life and perhaps with stronger energies – 'there were giants in those days' – but sparer, less detailed. It was Defoe who, in prose fiction, first brought to attention the usefulness and interest of a multiplicity of detail, and he was writing in an age when the growing scientific consciousness of men was teaching them to realise that no details were beneath their attention. Even Defoe did not apply this use of detail directly to characterisation, though Richardson began to, and Jane Austen mastered it. From Jane Austen to Joyce, the novel was marked by an increasingly close psychological texture, though the degrees and modes of it varied greatly from writer to writer, until Lawrence, who was as much a master of detail as anyone, disturbed readers by trying to recover the great, unifying simplicities, and critics declared that he could not create character. That was not true, but it is true that he was not always successful in finding words for what he sought. Will they ever be found? As yet there has been no further promise.

Index

Archers, The, 16
Austen, Jane, 16, 131, 136, 139-
140, 147, 155, 191, 199,
202
Novels:
Emma, 117-24, 132-4, 135,
173
Mansfield Park, 118
Northanger Abbey, 118
Sense and Sensibility, 98, 118
Characters in the novels:
Bates, Miss, 120, 121, 139,
140
Elton, Mr, 119, 122
Elton, Mrs, 121
Churchill, Frank, 118, 121,
123
Dashwood, Marianne, 118
Fairfax, Jane, 118, 121,
123
Knightley, Mr, 117, 122,
123
Morland, Catherine, 118
Woodhouse, Emma, 117-
124; compared to Cath-
erine Earnshaw, 132-4;
140, 141, 158, 188, 199

Brontë, Charlotte, 155
Jane Eyre, 13-14, 16
Brontë, Emily, 16, 141, 147,
200

Wuthering Heights, 124-34
Characters:
Dean, Nelly, 125, 132
Earnshaw, Catherine, 126,
128-9, 130; compared to
Emma Woodhouse, 132-
134; 140, 158, 188, 201
Earnshaw, Hareton, 129,
130, 133
Heathcliff, 127-31
Linton, Catherine, 126,
127, 129
Linton, Isabella, 125
Lockwood, 125
Bunyan, 23
Grace Abounding, 106
Pilgrim's Progress, 23, 24,
101-8
Characters:
Apollyon, 102, 103
Bubble, Madam, 107-8
By-ends, 104, 107
Christian, 101-7; com-
pared to Crusoe, 108-
114; 198, 201
Despondency, 104
Faithful, 102, 104, 106,
107
Fearing, 104
Feigning, Lady, 105
Giant Despair, 103
Greatheart, 103, 108
Honest, 104, 107

Bunyan—*continued*
Hopeful, 102, 104, 106, 107
Little Faith, 104
Muchafraid, 104
Pliable, 104, 107
Talkative, 103, 107
Worldly Wiseman, 106
Burton
Anatomy of Melancholy, 20

Chaucer
Canterbury Tales, 41
Romaunt of the Rose, 51
Troilus and Criseyd, 48-55
Characters:
Criseyd, 48-54; compared to the Wife of Bath (Alisoun), 54-5
Diomede, 53
Pandarus, 51
Troilus, 48-54
Conrad, 153
Cormican, L. A., 97

Danby, J. F., 82
Dante, 95-7
Defoe, 202
Robinson Crusoe, 24, 108-14
Serious Reflections of Robinson Crusoe, 114
Dickens, 16, 191
Dombey and Son, 162
Great Expectations, 156-63, 172-4, 179-80, 184, 190
Characters:
Biddy, 159, 160, 161, 162
Estella, 159, 162
Gargery, Joe, 158, 160-1

Havisham, Miss, 158, 159, 162
Jaggers, 160, 163
Magwitch, 161, 163
Pip, 156-63, 201
Pumblechook, 158, 173-4
Wemmick, 162-3
Dryden
Character of Achitophel, 20-2

Earle, John
Microcosmographie, 20
Eliot, George, 172, 200, 201
Middlemarch, 173
Daniel Deronda, 135-46, 154-155, 190
Characters:
Arrowpoint, Mrs, 137-9, 148
Deronda, 135, 146
Gascoigne, 144-6
Grandcourt, 142-4
Harleth, Gwendolen, 135-146; compared to Isabel Archer, 154-5; 188, 201
Everyman, as a character or character concept, 18, 19, 27, 28-33, 55, 68, 85, 97, 101-3, 201
Everyman (morality play), 27-33, 39-40

Forster, E. M., 155
Freud, 191

Garnett, Edward, 199
Gawayn and the Green Knight, 27, 33-40, 202

Hamlet, 19-20
Hardy, Thomas
  The Mayor of Casterbridge,
    163-72, 174-6
  Characters:
    Coney, Christopher, 174-6
    Cuxsom, Mother, 175-6
    Farfrae, Donald, 164-72
    Henchard, Michael, 163-
      172, 174-6, 201
    Henchard, Mrs, 170, 176
    Longways, Solomon, 174-6
    Lucetta, 168, 170
Hobbes
  Leviathon, 20

James, Henry
  The Portrait of a Lady, 146-55
  Characters:
    Archer, Isabel, 146-54;
      compared to Gwendo-
      len Harleth, 154-5; 188,
      201
    Goodwood, Caspar, 148
    Merle, Madam, 149, 151-
      153, 154
    Osmond, Gilbert, 149, 154
    Touchett, Ralph, 146, 148,
      150, 153
    Warburton, Lord, 148
Johnson, Samuel, 74
Joyce, James
  The Dubliners, 186
  Finnegans Wake, 18
  Ulysses, 179, 201
  *A Portrait of the Artist as a
    Young Man*, 177-87, 190

Characters:
  Cranly, 184-5
  Dedalus, Mr, 177, 179, 181
  Dedalus, Mrs, 177, 179
  Dedalus, Stephen, 177-87,
    191

Lawrence, D. H., 131, 155
  Women in Love, 187-98
  Characters:
    Brangwen, Gudrun, 188-9,
      190, 197, 198
    Brangwen, Ursula, 188-9,
      190
    Birkin, Rupert, 190-8
    Crich, Gerald, 190, 192,
      196-8
    Crich, Mrs, 188
    Loerke, 189
    Roddice, Hermione, 189
Leavis, F. R., 147, 154
Lewis, C. S.
  The Allegory of Love, 48, 53

Machiavellian character, 21
Meredith, 155
Milton
  Paradise Lost, 89-100
    Satan, 23, 24, 89-100, 114
  Mrs Dale's Diary, 16, 17

Nesbit, E.
  Treasure Seekers, 10-11

Picaresque character, 23, 101-
  114
Plutarch, 72, 73

INDEX

Potter, Beatrix
  Peter Rabbit, 9-10, 14

Quickly, Mistress, 176

Richardson, Samuel, 202

Scott, 172
Shakespeare, 19, 24, 141, 176
  Macbeth, 56-72, 99, 191
    Characters:
      Macbeth, 39, 59-66, 69-70

      Macbeth, Lady, 66-8, 69-70
      Duncan, 56-9
  Antony and Cleopatra, 72-85, 99
    Characters:
      Antony, 71, 72-6, 82-5
      Cleopatra, 71, 76-85
      Octavia, 77
      Octavius, 75
social ego, 131, 133, 199
society, in relation to character, 22, 24, 97-100, 105-6, 108, 114, 117, 133-4, 199-202